This is Not New

Praise for *Curationism*:

"Balzer writes with zest, scepticism, and sly humour."
—Sheila Heti, author of *Pure Colour*

"An insightful, provocative and entertaining overview of many of the key issues in both art and cultural life today."
—*ArtReview*

"Best Art Books of the Year."
—Sky Gooden, *National Post*

This is Not New

Art, Culture, and the Promise of Change

David Balzer

First published 2025 by Pluto Press
New Wing, Somerset House, Strand, London WC2R 1LA
and Pluto Press, Inc.
1930 Village Center Circle, 3-834, Las Vegas, NV 89134

www.plutobooks.com

Copyright © David Balzer 2025

The right of David Balzer to be identified as the author of this work has been asserted in accordance with the Copyright, Designs and Patents Act 1988.

British Library Cataloguing in Publication Data
A catalogue record for this book is available from the British Library

ISBN 978 0 7453 4270 2   Paperback
ISBN 978 0 7453 4277 1   PDF
ISBN 978 0 7453 4276 4   EPUB

This book is printed on paper suitable for recycling and made from fully managed and sustained forest sources. Logging, pulping and manufacturing processes are expected to conform to the environmental standards of the country of origin.

Typeset by Stanford DTP Services, Northampton, England

Simultaneously printed in the United Kingdom and United States of America

EU GPSR Authorised Representative
LOGOS EUROPE, 9 rue Nicolas Poussin, 17000, LA ROCHELLE, France
Email: Contact@logoseurope.eu

Contents

Preface   vi

Prologue: Some Radicals   1
1. Culture Industry, Culture Wars   24
2. Natural Supernatural   46
3. The Whole Earth   76
Epilogue: Deeper Understanding   121

Notes   149

Preface

This book is a small, sideways consideration of the contemporary attitude toward the new and its origins within the West and its culture industry, all in inevitable relation to politics. My argument is unoriginal and should be uncontroversial. The West's culture industry—once popular culture, now all-embracing digital culture—cannot, on its own, effect lasting, equitable social change. It was not designed to. Contemporary culture and politics, increasingly merged, and built on thin, often outrageously insincere, promises of the new, are placeholders for such change. Cultural history and media theory proclaim this, over and over. The current state of things, however, gives us reasons to ignore and forget. This book is an act of remembering.

The new is an impossibly broad topic. In the contemporary West, the new has dissonance, which is at the heart of this book. The liberal left may critique limitless-growth capitalism as an outdated remnant of, say, white, heteropatriarchal modernism. Yet, faith in and fascination with the new—as behaviour, method, framework, tone, and mindset—persist among progressives. When I began writing this book, hot topics included the Green New Deal, the "new voices" of diversity, equity, and inclusion initiatives, and the "unprecedented" events of Donald Trump's presidency and the COVID-19 pandemic. Each topic, now thoroughly critiqued, was never strictly new, but rather a combination of historical recurrence with present circumstance, the rote valuation of "new" lending an urgent, vital hue.

The backlash against such valuations, including the prevalence of the phrase "this is not new" in culture and news media, is one of the occasions for this book. Growing exhaustion with the new is not necessarily conservative. It is a reaction to a culture that relentlessly touts the new as best, while serious, long-standing problems persist. As a rallying cry, "new" is not an undoing or a revelation. It emerges, myth-like, to prop up the culture industry that touts it. This book does not itemize the authenticity of retro styles, the symptoms of cultural amnesia, or the problematics of appropriation. Rather, it looks at the under-discussed structures of such things—the machinery of the new, as meaning-generator.

This is not a handbook for social change. Such an intention would contradict the very nature of the project. I speak to our charged cultural moment when I say that this is only one book, relying as it does on my own point of view, pretending neither to be novel, shocking, comprehensive, nor, as a thinky book published by a leftist press, above what it critiques. This book cannot remake the culture industry of which it is a part.

This book intends ambivalence toward, not a polemic against, the culture industry. As a culture writer and a gay man, I have been shaped, delighted, trained, transfixed, and resourced by this industry—through films, music, books, art, and more. I know intimately of culture's power to situate, form, and transform. The pressure many put on culture makes deep sense to me.

Yet, we are now saturated with creative-expressive ways of seeing, doing, and being. Digital culture has made us into data to be managed, interpreted, and consumed. Culture does so much—too much. Art's old promise of eternal life for its creators grimly remains, accessible to millions: our digital selves will most certainly outlive us. Meanwhile, professionalized creativity is the pursuit of so many, and subject to a consumer cycle so fickle, rapid, and dispersed, that the results are difficult to parse and discern, let alone remember.

It was perhaps ever thus. Western culture is a churning cycle of creation and destruction, its democratic spirit haunted by class stratification and resource scarcity, and informed by an odd, contradictory idea of "new," which finds its roots both in Judeo-Christian and pagan belief. The West's culture industry is mighty, but inherently unfair. It wants always to draw attention *here* and not *there*, then *there* and not *here*. When it takes the wheel of progressive politics, it tends to go in circles.

Just as the Jamaican-British cultural theorist Stuart Hall, in his 1987 essay "Gramsci and Us," criticized the left of his day for its attachment to flattened notions of seizing the means of production—"all we see is capitalism disintegrating," wrote Hall, "and us marching in and taking over"[1]—so, in this book, I track the flattening of Italian philosopher Antonio Gramsci's notions of counter-hegemony, a hangover of the New Left of which Hall was a part. Gramsci's legacy has resulted in an overemphasis, by an increasingly fragmented left, on the culture industry as a site of radicality and revolution. Hall himself saw this fomenting in the 1980s, when neoliberalism, reaching across the political spectrum, began to use culture not for equitable change but to prevent such change from ever happening again. Now thoroughly neoliberal, the culture industry repackages radical thought as a substitute for policy reform, organizing, and direct action. "They say we need new images to help our movement grow," sang the British musician Robert Wyatt in 1985's "Age of Self." "And it seems to me if we forget / Our roots and where we stand / The movement will disintegrate / Like castles built on sand."[2]

* * *

Preface

I was born in Winnipeg, a city in a part of the Canadian Prairies that is also known as Treaty One Territory and Métis Country. I am from a Ukrainian Mennonite family that has been in Canada for almost two generations. Much of this book was written a hundred kilometers west of Toronto, on the Haldimand Tract, land along the Grand River that rightly belongs to the Six Nations—a fact certainly relevant to the (not) new.

I am not an academic. I have not set out to contribute anything novel to any field. If you are looking for an expert's take on the new, you have come to the wrong place. This book is composed in snapshot or collage style, digesting select histories and writings, while at the same time trying not to be epigrammatic or reductive. It is for the educated, general reader. It is especially for those with an interest in the culture industry's structures, functions, and limits; for culture workers with ever-dwindling resources expected to accomplish ever-lofty political tasks; and for anyone who cringes at the products, ideas, or phenomena of contemporary culture that claim to be new, and are plainly not.

It is a fool's errand to publish a book of cultural criticism that remains of-the-moment to the date of publication. Non-fiction books should not resemble editorials or thinkpieces with compressed turnaround times, meant for viral sharing and immediate reaction. The purview of this book thus ends somewhere around 2021. Its primary focus is what has become known as "the before time," that is, pre-COVID-19, in most cases decades before then. This book understands events from the late 2010s as recent history. The pandemic and its aftermath have undoubtedly changed the contemporary world. Here, I consider how the culture industry offers armour *against* such disruptive change. If something in this book strikes a reader as unfashionable, I ask them to consider my thesis. Indeed, the taboo surrounding the unfashionable has always irritated and fascinated me in equal measure—and I am delighted to finally be publishing a book about it.

I am a fiction writer as well as a cultural critic. This book is a longform essay, which tells a kind of story. "Storytelling" has become an overused phrase in most professional fields. Often omitted is a component of my own favourite stories—ambiguity, abstraction, and selective nondisclosure, where the reader follows the author in a detective-like process of *thinking through*. I attempt this here; I feel the complexity of the topic deserves it. I defer to German-US philosopher Hannah Arendt (via Immanuel Kant), whose work provides an antidote to current orthodoxies on the new: "[T]he need to think can be satisfied only through thinking, and the thoughts which I had yesterday will satisfy this need today only to the extent that I can think them anew."[3]

This book has five sections. The Prologue is a fragmented history of the figure of the radical in Western culture. Chapter 1 defines and describes the Western culture industry, and how it came to be taken up by neoliberalism, which put culture wars in place of practical politics and media literacy. Chapter 2 surveys how the Western idea of the new became a post-Enlightenment phenomenon that worked to merge art, religion, science, and creativity. Chapter 3 looks at the use of the cultural new in the USA as a means of economic fortification, ending inevitably in Silicon Valley, with grave consequences for the contemporary self. The Epilogue is about the British musician Kate Bush, whose dark experiments with technology—a Romantic tale for the Postmodern Age—presage current discourses on artificial intelligence, or AI, and sum up the book's concerns. Throughout, the book places emphasis on contemporary art and fine-art history, fields smitten with the new, in which I have spent many years working as a critic, editor, educator, and publisher. Brief consideration of the law, my current area of study and practice, also appears.

Thanks to the Banff Centre for Arts and Creativity, where, in 2017, Peta Rake and Kristy Trinier generously gave me time to begin research and thinking; to the brilliant eleven students at Quest University, Squamish, British Columbia, who, in spring 2019, collaborated with me on the class "Thinking Like an Art Critic"; to the Canada Council for the Arts, who provided a Research and Creation grant for this book the same year; to Alex Molotkow and Haley Cullingham, for supporting earlier versions of the Epilogue; and to Jade Blair, for research assistance. Thanks to the many friends, colleagues, and professors who suggested and prompted reading and research, notably to Professor Gordon Christie, whose Jurisprudence class at the Peter A. Allard School of Law, University of British Columbia, inspired my positioning of culture alongside law in Chapter 1, and began with Naomi Mezey's "Law as Culture," as I do there. Special thanks to Pluto Press and to my devoted friend and editor David Shulman, who sends me texts like "I have unquestioning belief in you." And to Glee Walker and Bruce White, who gave me a home in which to finish this book when I thought I might not have one.

This book is, with profound love and respect, for Robert and Natasha, whose wisdom, support, and patience made it real. It is also for the mud puddle at the bottom of the stairs.

Prologue
Some Radicals

On October 25, 2019, protestors gathered outside the Vancouver Art Gallery under a large banner advertising an exhibition by the well-known US photographic artist Cindy Sherman. They were not protesting the exhibition but rather government inaction on climate change. It was a Fridays for Future strike, organized by local group the Sustainabiliteens, part of a global movement inspired by the young Swedish activist Greta Thunberg who was, that day, slated to appear. The sky was clear. The sun cast sharp, cold shadows. The winds were high, dangerously so according to Environment Canada, sucking in and puffing out the banner against the bones of the gallery's neoclassical columns. Two thousand kilometers south, the Santa Ana winds spread wildfires across Southern California.

Sherman is associated with the so-called Pictures Generation, a group of artists who, in 1980s New York, appropriated and in Sherman's case restaged images from film, TV, and advertising. (Critics have called this "appropriation art," meaning something different from how it might be understood today.) Sherman appears in many of her photographs, taking on female personae from visual culture and making herself deliberately ridiculous, kitschy, and grotesque, and/or implicating herself in the often-violent scenarios that have become familiar in Western depictions of women, particularly in Hollywood films. The image on the banner was Sherman's *Untitled #92* (1981), part of her *Centerfold* series, commissioned by *Artforum*'s then-editor Ingrid Sischy, who pulled it from publication fearing reader backlash. The photograph depicts Sherman on her hands and knees, looking up across the frame. The blue-green hue suggests nighttime. The figure seems to have fallen under a light, perhaps on dock planks, where her splayed fingers, slightly dirty, maybe bloody, steady her body. Her hair is wet. She is wearing what appears to be a schoolgirl's uniform: a collared white blouse, undone at the top, and tucked into a kilt. Her lips are parted. Her wide, slightly puffy eyes suggest panic, distress, hunger.

Untitled #92 was not the first artwork to be a backdrop to protests at the Vancouver Art Gallery (VAG). The VAG comprises an entire block in downtown Vancouver and, as a former provincial courthouse, has played host to a variety of public actions, from The Great Depression Relief Demonstration of 1938 to the We Demand gay-rights demonstrations of the 1970s. The current location of the VAG was established in 1983, also the year of Operation Solidarity, the largest political demonstration to date in British Columbia, which fought austerity measures promised by the newly elected Social Credit Party. As artist Stan Douglas has noted, the VAG officially opened at the retrofitted provincial courthouse on the same day as these protests, "effectively [shifting] the proprioceptive centre of Vancouver"[1] to the gallery, part of the then recently opened Robson Square complex. Historically and notoriously, Vancouver's political actions have been thwarted by urban planning that avoided the construction of public squares, placing City Hall in the suburbs. The open space of the courthouse has thus remained potent. For decades, protests have had banners advertising exhibitions as their backdrops, rarely remarked upon but, at times, strangely apposite. The tent city of 2011's Occupy movement, for instance, was staked under an advertisement for an exhibition of real-estate developer Michael Audain's collection. In 2012, anti-Northern Gateway pipeline protests were under an advertisement for

"Beat Nation," a group show about contemporary Indigenous artists' connections to hip hop and featuring an image of Cree, Tsimshian, Gitksan, and Métis artist Skeena Reece's performance *Raven: On the Colonial Fleet* (2010), in which the artist dresses as a warrior.

On the day of the Fridays for Future strike, protesters gathered on the steps underneath Sherman's image to hold tight and unfurl a variety of their own banners: a long, red-and-black Coast Salish motif; signs reading "WE DEMAND A CLIMATE RECOVERY PLAN" and a popular chant from the Fridays for Future movement, "WE ARE UNSTOPPABLE, ANOTHER WORLD IS POSSIBLE." The spectacle of Sherman's image seemed incidental next to another that strike organizers seemed to want to defuse, that of Thunberg herself. Media attention on Thunberg had ballooned since she began her own strikes outside the Swedish parliament in 2018. Subsequently the subject of multiple *New York Times* pieces, a *New Yorker* profile, and several international wall murals, Thunberg had recently travelled to New York via a carbon-neutral boat to speak at the United Nations, landing in September to much media fanfare, to which she responded, "slightly embarrassed" according to a CBS News report: "all of this is very overwhelming."[2] Media coined the term The Greta Effect to describe Thunberg's influence on climate activism, especially among youth. Thunberg had found herself a symbol of the new: conquistador, meteorological phenomenon, and import all at once.

Months later, in December 2019, Thunberg, alongside German activist Luisa Neubauer, told a UN climate meeting in Madrid that "there is no need to listen to us anymore… It is people especially from the global south, especially from Indigenous communities, who need to tell their stories."[3] In Vancouver, despite chants of "Greta, Greta, Greta," she appeared last, after an extensive march through the city. Some crowd members, waiting for Greta, whispered impatiently to each other; some left. Indigenous land and water defenders Kanahus Manuel, of the Secwepemc and Ktunaxa Nations, and Audrey Siegl, of the Musqueam Nation, spoke of their decades-long, and their communities' centuries-long, fights. "I am grateful you are here," said Siegl to protestors. "But I wonder, where were you 50 years ago, 10 years ago? Where were your ancestors?"[4]

Thunberg finally emerged with Severn Cullis-Suzuki, daughter of Canadian environmentalist and media personality David Suzuki. Cullis-Suzuki had spoken at the Rio Climate Summit in 1992, at age 12, in a speech with unmistakable parallels to Thunberg's rhetoric, particularly in its pointed address to adults. "Severn told the world everything the world needed to know 27 years ago,"[5] Thunberg said to the crowd after quoting Cullis-Suzuki's speech, which also contains the lines, not quoted by Thunberg that day: "If you don't know how to fix it, please, stop breaking it."[6] Several months after the Vancouver strike, Cullis-Suzuki appeared on the BBC World Service podcast *The Real Story* with other young climate-justice activists. "When we started, we thought that people wouldn't be interested in our message," she told host Paul Henley. "[But] we actually got attention because we were young."[7] Henley's introduction to the episode noted that youth activism was "nothing new,"[8] citing the Soweto uprising in South Africa and more recent gun-control actions in the USA. "Can young people succeed where adults have failed?"[9] he asked guest Julianne Viola, an academic researcher who, in response, calmly pointed to the 1961 Greensboro sit-in where Ezell Blair Jr., Franklin McCain, Joseph McNeil, and David Richmond helped launch the US Civil Rights movement.

A year before the Rio Climate Summit, Cindy Sherman was getting bored of herself. According to a 1991 *Guardian* feature by British journalist Judy Rumbold, the artist, who was "a photographer, model, muse, costume designer, and makeup artist simultaneously,"[10] was concerned her image had become redundant. "People are finding it too entertaining,"[11] Sherman told Rumbold of her self-portraits, echoing a problem other successful Pictures Generations artists had had, where their art began to be consumed in the same way as the media culture it parodied and deconstructed. "She is considering the idea of a new series where she will not feature,"[12] Rumbold writes of Sherman. "Instead, dismembered limbs will better convey the horror of 'futuristic post-holocaustal decomposition.'"[13] Sherman's *Disasters* series from the late 1980s had in fact already done this. In 1992, Sherman unveiled her *Sex Pictures* series, comprising doll parts and prostheses, in which she was also absent. In a 1996 *October* magazine essay titled "Obscene, Abject, Traumatic," US critic Hal Foster groups these Sherman works with those of US artists Mike Kelley, Andres Serrano, Kiki Smith, and others, calling this "the shit movement in contemporary art."[14]

* * *

Francisco José de Goya y Lucientes painted *Saturn Devouring His Son* (*Saturno devorando a su hijo*) in his 70s, between 1819 and 1823. He was deaf from an unknown recurring illness that may have been due to lead-paint poisoning. According to some scholars, he was suffering from periodic depression. Goya conceived of the painting privately, putting it on the papered walls of his summer house, known as "La Quinto del Sordo," the deaf man's place, across the Manzanares river to the west of Madrid.[15]

Saturn Devouring His Son was unseen by the public in the artist's lifetime, part of a series that has become known as *The Black Paintings*. Along with two other series, the *Caprichos* and the *Disasters of War*, all a likely influence on Sherman, *The*

Black Paintings—their subjects death, destruction, corruption, nastiness—are often thought to have disrupted the European tradition so thoroughly as to birth another: the modern, the avant-garde, even the punk. That *The Black Paintings* were literally painted over existing, unfinished, decorative-bucolic landscapes Goya had previously put on the walls of his home suggests the power of the new to erase what has come before.

Saturn Devouring His Son was not born of nothing. Goya had made a chalk sketch of the scene almost 20 years previous, possibly inspired by Flemish painter Peter Paul Rubens's more ornamental but no-less-horrifying version. Rubens derived his painting from a myth told over and over in permutations, his source probably Hesiod's *Theogony*, a Greek text from the 8th century BCE that presents a genealogy of the gods. Kronos, known as Saturn by the Romans, was a titan: father of the gods, including Zeus. Kronos was the unruly son of Gaia, the earth, and Ouranos or Uranus, the sky—also Gaia's son.

The story goes as follows. Kronos castrates Uranus with an iron sickle made by his mother, avenging the pain caused to her by Uranus, who has been hiding their one-eyed and many-limbed children in a cave, the Earth also being Gaia's body. The castration doesn't quite work. Uranus's decapitated genitals become the aftermath of a kind of action painting, spilling blood on Gaia and producing, among others, the Furies and the Nymphs. When Kronos tosses his father's genitals into the sea, they produce the foam on which Aphrodite, or Venus, is born. Kronos's chaotic rage continues in the scenes depicted by Rubens and Goya. There, Kronos is in the process of devouring the children he has subsequently had with his wife, Rhea, because he is terrified of a prophecy that one of their children, Zeus, will overthrow him. When Rhea finally births Zeus, she enlists Gaia's and Uranus's help to hide Zeus in a Cretan cave. Then, Rhea gives Kronos a stone wrapped in swaddling clothes, claiming it is Zeus, and Kronos duly swallows it. When Zeus matures, he tricks Kronos into vomiting up all his offspring, who are so grateful they gift Zeus his iconic thunderbolt. Accounts outside Hesiod have Zeus subsequently castrating Kronos, repeating a family tradition.

Goya's *Saturn* is not just difficult to witness as an image. It is difficult to see properly as a work, because it is painted mostly in smoky black, its digital reproduction on the Internet accordingly hazy and indefinite. The painting has been hanging in Madrid's Museo del Prado since the 1890s (Rubens's version is also there) and, according to British art historian Nigel Glendinning, was not much visited even into the 1930s, at which point it and the other *Black Paintings* steadily became icons of the horrors of the 20th century, spiritual forbears of, say, the works of Irish playwright Samuel Beckett, or the photos of Bergen-Belsen concentration camp.[16] As has frequently been remarked on, there is an apparent bluntness to the rendering of Saturn, a cartoonishness, that makes it even more shocking. Saturn stares wide-eyed at the viewer, his gaze panicked and hungry, his mouth an open void. His long, scraggly, grey hair and beard spill over his shoulders. His elbows are out, his hands in fists, meeting across his chest to clutch a corpse the length of his own torso, its buttocks ambiguously gendered, its upper half beheaded and flayed. Saturn is in a semi-squat, the human posture most often associated with shitting.

Glendinning pieces together the story of *The Black Paintings*' transfer, after Goya's death, from the walls of the Quinto to canvas. He calls the transfer of *Saturn Devouring His Son* "decidedly less successful" than the other *Black Paintings*, comparing it with early photographs of the Quinto as well as etchings. Contrast and definition are lost, he claims, with incorrect contours. Goya's supposed style might be the result of the restorer's clumsiness. The child, according to Glendinning, was probably "more sensitively painted" in the original, and "the restorer has also lost the curved line of the lid over the staring right eye." Most egregious: "In the restored painting [Saturn's] penis is strangely placed," Glendinning writes, "apparently sprouting and hanging down in an improbable fashion from the stomach with unlikely highlighting on the root. The photograph seems to suggest that the painting originally showed an erect or partially erect penis, with a highlight on the foreskin."[17] Saturn's boner is among Western art history's more significant dares, more so because it was almost lost to censorship, a type of castration mirroring that in Hesiod.

The story of how *Saturn Devouring His Son* and the other *Black Paintings* became new is the story the West tells of how radical artists make their innovative masterpieces. In a 2016 essay, Australian art historian Derek Allan interprets Goya's achievement through the famous analysis of another art historian, André Malraux, who, in 1950, before he became France's Minister of Cultural Affairs, wrote *Saturne: Le destin, l'art, et Goya*, where he argued that Goya's achievement with the *Black Paintings* was to take art past the Renaissance and into a post-humanist, faithless world, one "lit by a black sun."[18] According to Malraux, Goya's *Black Paintings* maintain "the link between atrocity and the timeless." They refuse to please an audience. "For the first time," Allan writes, "there has emerged a form of art that denies the significance of man and leaves nothing in its place... Doing so meant embarking on something utterly new."[19]

When Rubens and Goya had painted Saturn or Kronos, the figure was understood as an archetype for time. Yet the ancient Greeks had two words for time. *Chronos*, associated with Saturn or Kronos, referred to chronological time, *kairos* to deeper, subjective time—points of crisis at which the new, at an opportune moment, might emerge to thwart the inevitable. *Kairos* was possibly named after the minor deity Caerus, child of Zeus, who had one lock of hair by which he could be seized. *Kairos* is an important concept in the history of philosophy (consider the Latin poet Horace's oft quoted *carpe diem*, or seize the day), and remains a fascination of inspirational social-media posters and hit-radio rappers alike. The German philosopher Martin Heidegger, building on early Christian theology, wrote of *kairos* in his 1927 book *Being and Time*, his hopeful rendering of the opportune moment later soured by his association with fascism.

By the Renaissance, Saturn or Kronos became the more generalized figure of Father Time. His castration sickle became the harvest sickle and then, after industrialization, lost its natural association to become a slasher symbol of pure death. Saturn's child-devouring came to represent time's own devouring: first, a symbol of the inevitability of patriarchal succession, then, under liberal capitalism, of any individual's march toward death, which might come at any time. *Tempus edax rerum*, wrote the Roman poet Ovid in *The Metamorphoses*, during a period obsessed with the succession of emperors. The phrase is commonly translated as "time the devourer," but more accurately means "time, a glutton for things."[20]

There are several ironies and paradoxes here. Hesiod's, and by association Goya's, Saturn is not devouring successfully. This Saturn is terrified of being devoured by his own son, in desperate denial of his own demise, and is ultimately avenged. Goya's Saturn may indeed be a self-portrait of an aging artist, fated to be supplanted by the next hot thing. This is not how Malraux and Allan see it. Their Goya is *kairos*, not *chronos*. Their Goya has maintained the link between the profane and the timeless. Their Goya has resisted an audience's pleasure and left himself, creativity—his own transcendent legacy. In pursuit of the "utterly new," their Goya, facing death, seized the opportune moment of the chaos of the void. Their Goya is heroic, beating time to become immortal. Through a private gesture of horror—indeed, because of it—their Goya has succeeded beyond measure.

The group of Italian artists known as the Futurists were likely the first to be called avant-garde, although the term has its own tangled provenance. Those invested in a shorthand understanding of "avant-garde" as anti-establishment or as somehow otherwise good, in the radical sense—edgy, experimental, fun, fresh, young, chic, metropolitan, subversive, disruptive, whatever—have tended to downplay the term's less attractive associations. These include political extremism (including, of course, fascism), capitalism (the avant-garde's apparent enemy but also, through arts patronage, its vital friend), appropriation ("immature poets imitate; mature poets steal," wrote the British-US poet T.S. Eliot[21]), colonialism (the early 20th-century Parisian avant-garde used ceremonial African objects as material and inspiration), violence (US performance artist Chris Burden was hospitalized in 1971 as a result of a gunshot wound he inflicted on himself for an art project), and a fierce culture of hierarchy, competition, and exclusion (arbitrary taste-making is the hallmark of the art and fashion worlds, the avant-garde's busiest sites, long parodied in popular films such as *Ghost World* and *Zoolander*).

US anthropologist David Graeber and Jamaican-British art critic Edward Lucie-Smith have both stressed the roots of the term avant-garde in 19th-century French religious thinkers Henri de Saint-Simon and Auguste Comte, who borrowed the military idea of an "advance guard" or "vanguard" that described the first troops to go into battle.[22] For Saint-Simon, the avant-garde comprised the innovative artist-leaders of his New Christianity. The socialism of Saint-Simon would continue with the art-historical attribution of "avant-garde" to French painter Gustave Courbet, exiled for his involvement in the Paris Commune. For the Italian Futurists, "avant-garde" was neither here nor there as a self-description. Yet the

Oxford English Dictionary gives the first example of the term's usage in 1910, the year after the Futurists published their first manifesto, *The Founding and Manifesto of Futurism*, on the front page of Paris newspaper *Le Figaro*. By 1912, the French writer Guillaume Apollinaire was using the term to describe the Futurists' popular exhibition at Paris's Bernheim-Jeune Gallery.[23] The Futurists were connected with combat, with heightened awareness of how various birth- and death-states can be deployed, politically and aesthetically. They could be seen as anarchists. They were also directly and indelibly associated with fascism.

The Futurists were gory and lifeless all at once. It is hard to explain what the Futurists' work was all about aside from bombast, audacity, machismo, and nihilistic self-assertion. They championed technological innovation over anything old. At the same time, they called for a sort of primeval brutality, extrapolating on and fetishizing the so-called primitive. They fought tradition and civilization. They wrote dozens of manifestos and were interdisciplinary, associated with poetry, painting, sculpture, theatre, dance, fashion, architecture, more. *Avant la lettre*, they were a think tank, a moving factory, a start-up, influencers. Their provocative *serata*, a series of public cultural demonstrations, were an arguable template for the happenings of the 1960s and for performance art in general. They were a model for other such agglomerations of the modernist avant-garde in Russia, Germany, France, and elsewhere.

If the Futurists were the first popular avant-gardists—they were not, as US scholar Jed Rasula points out, the first "Futurists," for Majorcan writer Gabriel Alomar had coined the term in 1904, five years before the Italian group's first manifesto[24]—they were also the first in the avant-garde's ruthless history to go irrelevant, stale, passé. The Futurists did significant work to innovate such a fate. The audacity of their de facto leader, Filippo Tommaso Marinetti, now looks, not menacing, but either purposely self-defeating or like so much buffoonery.

In 1981, the US critic Rosalind Krauss, champion of Sherman's Pictures Generation, wrote an essay for *October* magazine titled "The Originality of the Avant-Garde and Other Modernists Myths," in which she argued against the claims to originality of groups like the Futurists. Krauss's mockery of Marinetti touches on his and the Futurists' noted misogyny. She writes of his much-cited description, in the first manifesto, of a car accident: "thrown from his automobile," Krauss writes, "one evening in 1909 into a factory ditch filled with water, [and emerging] as if from amniotic fluid to be born—without ancestors—a futurist."[25] Like the other male modernists after him, Marinetti wanted to be a by-product of Saturn's father-castration, to come into existence totally new and without the aid of a bodily womb, by way of the ditches of industry. As US scholar Lawrence Rainey notes, the title character of Marinetti's novel, *Mafarka the Futurist*, written the same year as the first Futurist manifesto, "[conquers] several kingdoms in northern Africa"—Marinetti was born in Alexandria, Egypt—"renounces them to 'become a builder of mechanical birds!' and so '[gives] birth to [his] son without the help of the vulva!'"[26]

At the end of her essay, Krauss asserts that "the historical period the avant-garde shared with modernism is over," and that, by the early 1980s, the "fictitious condition" of modernism's claim to originality was being exposed as "splintering into endless repetition."[27] Krauss concludes, and undercuts, her essay with an effective endorsement of Sherrie Levine, a Pictures Generation artist who made unabashed, obvious reproductions of canonical artworks and, in Krauss's opinion, "seems most radically to question the concept of origin and with it the notion of originality."[28] Here, Krauss separates her own idea of the avant-garde (postmodern, perhaps) from modernism's apparent problem—its attachment to the most distasteful, disturbing aspects of the new. Yet, with Levine as her solution, Krauss touts the new in an old way, putting a fresh, self-conscious Pictures Generation product in place of dated, supposedly unselfconscious modern ones.

(Krauss herself was born an art-historical academic through a car crash. "I was in fact thinking of a [thesis] topic in nineteenth-century European art that would have been much more palatable to my professors at Harvard," she told US gallerist Judy K. Collischan Van Wagner in the 1984 anthology *Women Shaping Art: Profiles of Power*:

> I didn't know what to do until one morning I woke up to an announcement on my clock radio that a sculptor had been killed in Vermont. I thought it was Tony Caro, because they said "Bennington, Vermont," where he was teaching. I thought, "Oh, how terrible," because I knew Tony. Then, after a couple of sentences, they repeated the name and I realized that it was [David] Smith. I thought, "Um, I now have a thesis topic." I knew they would never allow me to do a dissertation of somebody who was still alive, but he had just died. I went rushing to Harvard to announce this as my topic.[29])

In US novelist Rachel Kushner's 2013 novel *The Flamethrowers*, set in the time in which Krauss wrote "Originality" and written in a time in which conceptual art from this period resurged in popularity as a backdrop to social-media selfies, a nameless female artist—known only as "Reno" because she comes from Reno, Nevada—navigates the New York art world. Reno's boyfriend is Sandro Valera, a successful, unfeeling Italian artist who makes, or rather has manufactured, things like "aluminum boxes, open on top, empty inside."[30]

Valera is the scion of a Marinetti-esque industrialist. Kushner begins her novel with the Latin epigraph *FAC UT ARDEAT*. In an interview with the *Paris Review*, Kushner explained that the epigraph came from an inscription she saw above the fireplace in the "childhood home of an Italian friend who came out of a Fascist background."[31] The full quotation is derived from the 13th-century Latin hymn to the Virgin Mary's suffering, the *Stabat Mater*: *Fac ut ardeat cor meum in amando Christum Deum* (Make my heart burn with love for Christ). Although Kushner's friend had thought *Fac ut ardeat*, made to burn, had some association with fascist insurrection, Kushner realized it could just be a joke about the fireplace's function.

By the end of Kushner's art-world parable, the reader sees the epigraph as a dark joke about the avant-garde itself. Any of its gestures is made to burn: fleeting, combustible, reduced to ash. Any threat posed by the avant-garde is not lastingly socio-political. If it stays at all, it stays in the art world, a closed economy. "Gordon Matta-Clark just cut an entire house in half," says a taunting male artist to Reno at the end of a night of partying, about the famed 1970s conceptual artist. "It's going to be tough to beat that. What now, Reno? What now?"[32]

Fac ut ardeat is a stark Futurist truth, expressed in many of the movement's works and borne out by the movement's very trajectory. There is certainly bravado in the first Futurist manifesto, but this includes creative futility and self-destruction, unmistakably rooted in a death drive. We are expendable, we will be forgotten, and we don't care. Marinetti writes:

> The oldest of us is thirty: so we have at least a decade left to fulfill our task. When we are forty, others who are younger and stronger will throw us into the wastebasket, like useless manuscripts.—We want it to happen!

> They will come against us, our successors; they will come from far away, from every direction, dancing to the winged cadence of their first songs, extending predatory claws, sniffing doglike at doors of the academies for the good smell of our decaying minds, long since promised to the libraries' catacombs.
>
> But we won't be there. ...They will find us, at last—one wintry night—in an open field, beneath a sad roof drummed by monotonous rain, crouched beside our trembling airplanes and in the act of warming our hands by the dirty little fire made by the books we are writing today, flaming beneath the flight of our imaginings.[33]

The Futurists place the gesture of the new not in private but in the amnesia of the crowd and its technological fancies. From public spectacle to garbage, the Futurists aimed to leave nothing for successors except a subliminal pattern of attempt. How else can the new be furnished, Marinetti implies, except by making room through annihilation—burning? "Our houses will last less time than we do," writes Futurist Antonio Sant'Elia in *Futurist Architecture* (1914), like a cynical condo developer. "Every generation will have to make its own city anew."[34]

Futurism declined with less glamour than its first manifesto predicted. Rainey tells of Marinetti's visit to US émigré artist-writers Gertrude Stein and Alice B. Toklas's salon during the Futurists' 1912 Paris exhibition, about which Toklas writes, "in any case everybody found the futurists very dull."[35] This comment may well be relevant to the Futurists' noted anti-Semitism and misogyny—Stein and Toklas, Jewish lesbians, were likely wary—but also shows the ever combative and cliquey nature of the avant-garde, due in no small part to the tentative, fragile, and territorial nature of the utterly new. By 1920, Marinetti had withdrawn from active involvement in fascism to work on his art, devising another Futurist sub-movement called Tactilism, comprising activities that, according to Rainey, pertained to the "discovery of new senses" that would "carry the human spirit to unknown shores." When Marinetti went to Paris again to lecture about Tactilism, the press was as underwhelmed as Toklas. Parisian avant-gardists Tristan Tzara and Francis Picabia, associated with the surrealist and Dada movements, distributed a leaflet at the lecture reading, "Futurism has died... From what? From DADA."[36]

Marinetti lived well past 40, into his late 60s. "The oldest of us is thirty" was a lie. Marinetti was past 30 when the first Futurist manifesto was written. By the early 1920s, Marinetti had married artist Bernadetta Capa and settled down, eventually having three daughters. In 1929, Benito Mussolini inaugurated a Royal Academy and recruited several faculty for it, each paid generously. Marinetti, who played a role in Mussolini's rise, was one. Short-term risk had yielded long-term gain. Rainey writes: "that Marinetti had once urged the closure of all arts academies was a contradiction every critic, ever since, has felt obliged to note."[37] (Marinetti's call to burn the museums was not new, at least as a critical wish. In Volume I of *Modern Painters* [1843], British critic John Ruskin wrote of the "lower" Dutch landscape artists: "I conceive the best patronage that any monarch could possibly bestow upon the arts, would be to collect the whole body of them into a grand gallery and burn it to the ground."[38])

In 1932, the administrative council for the Venice Biennale complained about the space given to the Futurists year after year. Rainey recounts the transcript of the exchange among council members. "But, must there always be a Futurist room?" asks Margherita Sarfatti, to which Antonio Maraini answers, "Marinetti has asked me this year for no less than four or five rooms." They laugh. "It would be good to decide, once and for all, that the Futurists must meet the same standards as all the others," continues Maraini. Cipriano Oppo says: "In Rome [at the Quadriennale] we were inspired by the same ideas just expressed by Maraini, and we limited the number of Futurists to three or four. But Marinetti wrote to [Mussolini], who called me and told me to add an additional eight. ... It is blackmail."[39]

* * *

In 1994, a special section of *Performing Art Journal* (*PAJ*) called "Ages of the Avant-Garde" was dedicated to a series of testimonials by US avant-garde artists who "had turned fifty or older in the 18 years in which *PAJ* has chronicled the changing arts and politics of the 'downtown' scene, centred in [New York neighbourhoods] the Village and Soho."[40] Among them was writer and playwright Richard Foreman, then age 55:

> But it seems to be that getting older in the context of a culture that is hostile to the avant-garde, but decidedly NOT hostile to youth, means that the avant-garde is in America often confused with youth—hence the current assertions that various manifestations of pop-drug-edge culture have absorbed the avant-garde and/or made it irrelevant.[41]

Foreman contends that the avant-garde is about rejecting art that covers up the "basic energies" of fear and death, so that "getting old, within the context of the avant-garde, means therefore getting closer to the subject one originally dared to broach." In becoming a not-new body, Foreman is new again. "I don't fear senility," he says, "because I sense it as a kind of final 'pruning' that allows a final, rarest blossom to flower. I who in my youth HATED flowers."[42]

The "pop-drug-edge culture" to which Foreman refers is of course hardly divorced from fear of death. At least since Romanticism, youth-driven aesthetics in the West have had an unmistakable death drive, well documented in 20th-century popular music, which, well before the Internet, was understood through viral terminology such as "catchy" and "craze." Did the Futurists presage rock 'n' roll?

By Foreman's time, the avant-garde came to be understood as having a theoretical definition taken from Marxism, although in obvious parallel with Marinetti. Avant-gardists were attempting to move art from its traditional, bourgeois context—objects of idle contemplation in galleries and theatres with limited or no power to transform society—into "praxis," or industrial society's day-to-day, always-productive life, to provoke and perhaps revolutionize. For the US conceptual artist Lee Lozano, for instance, not talking to women and not participating in the art world's various openings were the artworks *Decide to Boycott Women* and *General Strike Piece*, respectively. A better question, perhaps: did rock 'n' roll, a product of the culture industry to be consumed by Baby Boomer youth, ever become, or intend to become, praxis?

British Invasion bands penned many songs about sad old people, gazing both without and within: The Beatles' "Eleanor Rigby," the Zombies' "A Rose for Emily" (inspired by US writer William Faulkner's short story about a woman who sleeps with her husband's corpse), the Who's "Pictures of Lily," the Kinks' "Well-Respected Man" (and many others), and the Rolling Stones' "As Tears Go By" (and many others). Such songs are not only carefree, ageist snubs, but also anxious, class-based expressions about joining the establishment and then dying—mentally, then physically. Such British Invasion bands claimed to speak the truth about death to the bourgeoisie, leaning on writers who set the stage for the Western avant-garde: Russian novelists Fyodor Dostoevsky and Nikolai Gogol and European philosophers Jean-Paul Sartre and Friedrich Nietzsche, the latter of whose ideas on the sacred and profane are present in Futurist thought and appear throughout this book.

In 1964, the Stones' "As Tears Go By" told of a sad old person watching children playing at dusk, "doing things I used to do / they think are new."[43] Originally titled "As Time Goes By," this was the first song Keith Richards and Mick Jagger wrote together, and has since become an ironic emblem of the Stones' own career as unrelenting, constantly touring Baby Boomer rockers. The most interesting story of "As Tears Go By" is, however, of Marianne Faithfull, who had a bigger hit with it, becoming, as a beautiful young woman, a novelty along with her death-haunted song. If the Stones and other British bands had appropriated and repackaged Black rhythm and blues to arrive at their novelty, Faithfull's femininity was repackaged and appropriated in turn.

In her autobiography, Faithfull explains the story of "As Tears Go By" as the tale of her "life proper" in "Pop Mythology."[44] Instead of crawling out of a ditch and being reborn a Futurist, Faithfull was "discovered" at a party by producer Andrew Loog Oldham, who said numerous times of her, "I saw an angel with big tits and signed her."[45] When Faithfull tried to tell her boyfriend at the time that she had essentially become a pop star overnight, they were sitting at a café and, before she could say anything, her hit came on the radio, acting as her voice and saying it all before she could. A few years later, in French director Jean-Luc Godard's *Made in U.S.A.*, Faithfull would re-stage this scene, making a cameo by sitting beside the actor Anna Karina in a café and repeating the song, acapella, as if she had turned into a (broken) jukebox. In the late 1980s, when Faithfull was in her 40s, she rerecorded "As Tears Go By" for her spare album *Strange Weather*, her voice octaves lower and soaked with character after years of drug use and hard living, the aesthetic aftermath of her early fame. She had transformed from a culture-industry novelty into an avant-garde artist-cum-artwork, closer, per Foreman, to her subject as she aged. She was rock as praxis.

Other Baby Boomer musicians in the 1980s grappled with aging after their youth-oriented fame. Settling down to become bourgeois, as Marinetti had done, was a countercultural theme as early as 1970, when Crosby, Stills, Nash & Young released "Our House," a song written by Graham Nash about going domestic in Los Angeles's Laurel Canyon with fellow singer-songwriter Joni Mitchell. (At the time of the song's release, Mitchell had already left Nash. According to her own Pop Mythology tale, Mitchell had announced her intention via a Western Union telegram from Greece: "If you hold sand too tightly, it will run through your fingers."[46]) By 1989, "Our House" was being used to advertise Sears Kenmore appliances on TV. That same year, Don Henley, of the popular 1970s band The Eagles, released his song "The End of the Innocence," and singer-songwriter Billy Joel, who had just turned 40, released his song "We Didn't Start the Fire." Both made the Billboard top ten, with Joel's song going to number one by the year's end.

The genre these two songs were associated with, adult contemporary or soft rock, was relatively new at the time, but hardly seen as avant-garde. Still, the songs suggest passivity in the face of decay that recalls the first Futurist Manifesto. In Henley's devastating song, a social critique of the Reagan administration, he sings, in the verses, of environmental catastrophe, the military-industrial complex, and 1980s power lawyers, in the chorus issuing a melancholy invitation to his lover to get lost in the nostalgia of their mutual 1950s upbringing, a drug-like coping mechanism. "Just lay your head back on the ground," he sings. "And let your hair fall all around me / Offer up your best defense / But this is the end... of the innocence."[47]

In Joel's better-known song, he presents the listener with a litany of cultural-political events, texts, and figures from the 40 years of his life: Buddy Holly, Marilyn Monroe, Lawrence of Arabia, the Belgian Congo, Adolph Eichmann, the Iranian Revolution, etc. The song remains best known for its chorus, a shameless Baby Boomer move to innocence. "We didn't start the fire," Joel sings. "It was always burning since the world's been turning / We didn't start the fire / No, we didn't light it but we tried to fight it."[48] Like the Futurists, Henley and Joel warm their hands at the fire fed by the flight of youthful imaginings. In Henley, it is a dying flame, in Joel, a raging bonfire. In both, it is beyond the artist's control.

* * *

In February 2020, on the escalating cusp of the global COVID-19 pandemic, the US-Canadian musician Grimes released the album, *Miss Anthropocene*. It was, in her words at the time, "an evil album about how great climate change is," in which she would play the titular villain she invented, whose name is a pun mixing "misanthropy" with "anthropocene," the latter the contested geological term for our current era, characterized by human impact that includes but is not limited to climate change. Grimes told *Crack* magazine in advance of the album release:

> The way I figure it is that climate change sucks and no one wants to read about it because the only time you hear about it is when you're getting guilted... I wanted to make climate change fun. *Miss Anthropocene* has got a Voldemort kind of vibe. She's naked all the time and she's made out of ivory and oil. It's going to be super tight.[49]

She went on:

> My Instagram bio was: "I pledge allegiance to the robot overlords" for, like, two years. I thought people understood that I ultimately probably believe in an AI dictatorship. I mean, I don't think humanity is going to survive anyway. We're fucked. I think AI is the natural evolution. It's just like we killed the fucking Neanderthals, and now they're going to kill us. I don't think democracy really works. These are the kinds of things I think. I actually, for the short term, am a bit of a socialist, but not economically. I'm into free markets. What can I say? I think capitalism can solve some things.[50]

How an AI dictatorship will be powered in a resource-scarce world is something Grimes and her interviewer did not address.

If the nihilism of *Miss Anthropocene* had ties to Futurism, it could not have happened without the Internet. Since 2018, when Grimes had gone public about her relationship with billionaire South African entrepreneur Elon Musk, Grimes has been seen with ambivalence by music critics and long-time fans alike. It wasn't just climate change or developing AI that had altered things for her during her five-year break between albums. Cancel culture had happened, in which people are named, online, for alleged bad behaviour and thereby compelled to atone and/or resign from social media, employment, more.

Grimes hadn't been cancelled. She was too rich, famous, and institutionally unaffiliated for that. But she had become and remains synonymous with backlash, a putative betrayer of the goth-electro values of her early days. On *Miss Anthropocene*, Grimes included the song "Delete Forever," named after the prompt Google's Gmail gives to spam. She claimed the song was about friends who had died from opioid addiction. It doubled as commentary on the vulnerability of anyone's virtual self, hers included. At 31, the same age Marinetti was when he was pulled from the ditch, Grimes had deleted herself to be born again.

1
Culture Industry, Culture Wars

> These Reaganomics are killin' my stomach,
> I feel like I've got to vomit,
> You voted Republican and Democratic too,
> Now I don't know just what to do,
> You voted for Reagan, and you voted for Bush,
> Now we all got to take a look,
> Come we, come woe,
> *Status quo*,
> This old stuff has got to go.
>
> —"Status Quo" (1983) by US rapper Donald Banks, reputedly written by former US Civil Rights lawyer W. Edward Thompson

How does one define the popular, mediated culture of the West? How well do those who consume and work within such culture understand its nature and purpose?

I asked such questions more when I left culture work for law school. There, I was required to take a class on jurisprudence, the philosophy of law, which effectively starts from zero to ask, "What is this thing we call law?" During my humanities degrees, I was not required to take an equivalent class about art and culture. Indeed, no such class existed. This class, I imagined, would not be the same as the classes I had taken on post-structuralism. Rather, it would broadly consider the concept and essence of art and culture in the West. How have a variety of thinkers suggested art and culture function and coexist with other aspects of Western life? (Aesthetics, now a fringe discipline, only partly covers this.) How have such characteristics been systematized and professionalized by the Industrial Revolution and its aftermath?

Jurisprudence takes nothing about law for granted as true; could the same be done with culture? One might start with an under-recognized observation: that what has become the culture industry is not all there is to culture, just as what has become the legal system is not all there is to law. Yet, neither the culture industry nor the legal system is artificial in practice, or disconnected from its non-systemic forms. Whatever they are and wherever they appear, law and culture are not mere imaginaries. Just as those who encounter the legal system are profoundly shaped by it, and those with little to do with it may consider it an abstraction but are nonetheless shaped by it, the culture industry has made much meaning for millions of lives, regardless of engagement. As US-Palestinian scholar Edward Said wrote in his 1978 study *Orientalism*, about the West's creation of a corresponding idea of "East": "One ought never to assume that the structure of Orientalism is nothing more than a structure of lies or of myths which, were the truth about them to be told, would simply blow away."[1]

Law is a useful comparison with culture because law is, for most jurisprudence scholars, part of culture. US scholar Naomi Mezey's 2003 essay "Law as Culture" sets out a helpful building-block definition. Citing the late Welsh writer Raymond Williams, Mezey observes that culture as a concept in the West really developed in the 18th century, when it was used for social and economic distinctions.[2] Culture, generally, is composed of symbols, a system of signs, and is not fixed but complex, upholding various, contextual value systems. Mezey's shorthand definition of culture is any "shared, signifying practices" in which "meaning is produced, performed, contested, or transformed."[3] Mezey does not clearly distinguish between culture as industry and culture in its other forms. If Williams is to be believed, the distinction, in the West, may be moot. There, anyone who refers to culture generally is referring to a concept and energy that resulted in the Industrial Revolution.

Talking about culture through culture itself—an inevitability—requires caveats. This is the work of theory, a combination of relational thinking, proposition, and personal, lived experience. This is not a strict science. Culture writers compose essays and artists make art about the way things are, citing personal, anecdotal evidence, and/or research, which includes other, confirming theorists and artists. This is not hypocrisy if it does not claim to be totally objective. Consider the central questions of anthropology, the original cultural studies: can a culture ever be fully observed through fieldwork, in which a given culture is studied and described by someone from the outside? Isn't such observation better done by those living within the culture, because cultural meanings are shared and generated by social groups? The former is limited and potentially exploitative; the latter risks legibility and translation issues. Both risk bias. Like law, culture, industrial or otherwise, simply cannot, in any totally accurate way, be explained. One is never fully outside of it.

But the study of culture is not futile. Some jurisprudence scholars are positivists, asserting that the law is posited, that is, put into place by humans, and thus *can* exist and be studied with *some* objectivity. Law has become a thing, and we may study things. Legal positivists are not often associated with cultural studies theorists like Mezey. However, both understand that law and culture are products of society and are thus intelligible to it. In contemporary popular culture, with taste and identity playing such strong roles, a strict positivist approach to cultural analysis may seem to deny the changing morals and contexts within which culture operates. But strict positivism in jurisprudence is, arguably, never the aim of any serious legal theorist. Legal positivists do not deny the influence of morality and context on law, just as they do not use the scientific method to study the law. They are self-described theorists, who believe certain aspects of the law may be observed—within their approach.

It would not, therefore, behoove any competent cultural critic to see the culture industry as beyond *any* observation. There is the clear, binding context of this industry: capitalism. As the cultural studies field has long held, it is not advisable to ignore popular culture because it is the dominant culture under which many of us will live and die. In jurisprudence, the so-called modern natural law theorists, after World War II, argued that legal systems could only be law if they had sources such as values, morals, and ideals. Nazi officials who said they were merely following orders and acting legally were not, therefore, following "real" laws and so were acting extra-legally. For many years, capitalism was to culture as Nazism was to law. That is, capitalism was not a value, moral, or ideal; its popular culture could never be *real* culture. Times have changed. In the contemporary West, the value, moral, or ideal underlying the culture industry is obvious: liberalism. Its concepts of liberty and equality are at the root of contemporary capitalism and its obsessions with creativity, expression, and self-actualization. This includes the centrality of the new.

* * *

The term "culture industry" is associated with Max Horkheimer and Theodor Adorno, who wrote an essay about it in a complex, disturbing book published in German in 1947 called *Dialectic of Enlightenment*. In shortest form, the authors, writing during fascist terror and socialist failure, saw a dominant style of Enlightenment thinking—aka positivism, which, following the Protestant Reformation, upheld science, reason, and rigorous, dispassionate observation—as really motivated by the fearful, impossible human desire to completely control the unknown.

Horkheimer and Adorno's resistance to positivism is the "dialectic" of their title, a term from classical philosophy adapted by the 18th-century German philosopher Georg Wilhelm Friedrich Hegel, and then again by his compatriot Karl Marx. "Dialectic" refers to the pursuit of the essence or truth of an idea through the uncovering of its apparent opposite—a process meant to lead to enlightenment. *Dialectic of Enlightenment* approaches this path ironically. The authors argue that, by pretending to resist myth as superstitious, primitive, backward, and irrational, modern society hides what it has in common with myth: a futile ambition to make all things knowable. The culture industry typifies this dialectic, trading in myths, for example romantic stories, and in raw data or information, for example news media, both giving audiences the false impression that, by consuming this industry's products, they gain a worldview that explains everything and thus immunizes them from deception—the attitude, of course, of those easiest to deceive.[4]

The culture industry is the subject and title of an entire chapter in *Dialectic of Enlightenment* subtitled "Enlightenment as Mass Deception." Although the chapter is not cheery—it doubts any Western culture remains apart from a growing industry that peddles the useful, economic, and knowable—the authors do not yearn for a time when culture was ever freer or better. (Before art was in thrall to the culture industry, they note, it was in thrall to patrons.) The chapter's era-specific references have not survived—the most popular of popular culture tends not to—but its authors' deep pessimism is prescient, and difficult to convincingly explain away as cranky, or irrelevant to the digital era.

The authors argue that the culture industry is essentially a business in service of its customers' needs. Audience may be king, but it is not free. The culture industry is designed to maintain the position of those whose economic power is already the strongest, and does so by encouraging individuality, dialogue, freedom, and autonomy. Through media, the culture industry introduces new forms that claim to liberate, but end up constraining. First, the telephone, where people talked to each other over great distances; then, radio, where one person talked to many over great distances; then, TV, where images dominated speech.[5]

In every way, the culture industry extends the world of work into leisure.[6] Working people may use the culture industry to unwind, but they continue to work when they consume its products, praising or criticizing its celebrities, for instance, or making significant efforts to follow its detailed, puzzling plot points. This is not art but the structure of it, the authors argue—and it is not new. The West has always aimed to make art reproducible, and has long offered entertainment as a salve for class conflict.[7] The culture industry may make some critics yearn, uselessly, for something more authentic, but to speak of what culture is and should be is a way of making the culture industry stronger—because it is to speak of culture as a thing to be managed and administrated, of culture *as* industry. Well-organized resistance to the culture industry is simply "the trademark of those with a new idea to sell."[8]

The not-new is at the centre of the culture industry, whose products are all essentially the same. A book quickly becomes a movie, which quickly becomes a fashion line, and any distinction between these products is trivial. The culture industry rotates on the spot, its constant pulse ensuring that nothing new will ever happen. It is not that everything is meaningless. Rather, this industry must generate meaning and value in every detail. Culture with no purpose simply cannot be industrial culture. The culture industry makes constant offers and promises—coercive because they are vague and unverifiable, with the appearance of scientific certainty. Self-proclaimed experts thrive in this industry, in which apparent expertise is all there is.

The culture industry is crucially modelled on the individual, the self, which comes together in large groups—at the time of the authors' writing, the masses of the 20th century's mass media—and struggles to connect intimately, one-on-one. Cultural consumers are presented with many means to attain satisfaction but are still fed up. This malaise has, the authors note, much in common with fascism.[9] Advertising, for instance, dissolves boundaries between self/consumer and audience/industry. People come late to a film and cannot tell if they are watching a trailer or the feature. After, they speak to their friends and colleagues as if they are characters from the film, becoming advertisements for the film in an ironic assertion of their own uniqueness.

So enduring is "The Culture Industry: Enlightenment as Mass Deception" that it appears not to predict but simply to describe any number of contemporary phenomena: Web 2.0 as the TV to the early Internet's telephone; thought, speech, and sight reduced to social-media posts (seeing in the form of Instagram posts, for example); the grip of work on all aspects of life; the "croudwork" phenomenon, in which users of apps like Airbnb and Uber are both consumer and employer; distraction and the so-called attention economy; the advent of reality TV; creativity as the economic baseline of artistic expression; "radical chic," liberal culture's uncanny ability to absorb, fund, and sell political resistance; Hollywood's preoccupation with many-times-reheated intellectual property, its risk-aversion to original content; the positioning of cultural products as socially useful (e.g., "this is the film/album/etc. we need right now"); gamification, or the designing of products and experiences in the form of games, which are really forms of work; expert culture and the professionalization of all creative endeavours; the development of AI to such an extent that it may replace professional activities, such as graphic design, film production, and academic writing, which were templated and mechanistic to begin with; digital culture's centering of the self via surveillance; advertising as a complete way of being in the world; subcultures and fandoms who labour to identify and value a set of cultural products that seem, to outsiders, very much the same; microtrends, microgenres, and microcelebrities; and, overall, the persistence of a certain type of newness, which consumers call new, but know is not new at all.

* * *

The German-South Korean philosopher Byung-Chul Han's 2010 work *The Burnout Society* argues that the West is no longer defined by a disciplinary society designed to keep things out, but a consumer, or "achievement," society, designed in every sense to let things in.[10] We are, in Han's opinion, too wide open.

Han's initial metaphor is pathological. Disciplinary society seeks to immunize against invaders, seen as pathogens. Achievement society is about neurons. The distinction is negative versus positive. The West, the world, may seem more viral than ever, but it is not very immunological. Our obsession with permission is just another form of work, in which we manage the default state of being so wide open. Online culture welcomes virality, for instance, yet cancel culture requires hypervigilance and paranoia—the digital self as always available, never fully controllable. During COVID-19, liberal and conservative cultures alike fixated on mask-wearing—social productivity as permission—and on vaccines—surrendering the body to the wisdom of science and the pharmaceutical industry.

In Han's achievement society, one must always say yes. The self is a liberal subject *ad absurdum* and must work hard to actualize, but never at the expense of anyone's or anything's freedom, especially not the market's. The results are the hallmark disorders of our time, boundary-related and neurological: attention-deficit hyperactivity disorder (ADHD), borderline personality disorder (BPD), burnout, and depression.[11]

Enlightenment positivism has become dystopic. The call to observe and analyze everything makes rationality impossible. The root of the English word "positive," from the Old French *positif* and the Latin *positivus*, generally means to put a system in place, echoing the legal positivists and explaining the legal term "dispositive"—when something, such as a piece of evidence, determines a case. For Han, so much is put into place that nothing can be determined. The late British writer Mark Fisher saw depression or anhedonia, the inability to feel pleasure, as emblematic of a contemporary world where people are so resigned to capitalism that they have "the morose conviction that nothing new can ever happen."[12] Han describes something different. His depressive is "a new human type," so overexposed that they have dropped all defenses to "become predator and prey at once."[13] Han's depressive isn't pessimistic about the new but defenseless against it. The *Oxford English Dictionary* defines "positive" with the phrase "admitting no question"—suggesting discipline but also its opposite, total acquiescence.

Accelerated productivity, a nightmarish residue of positivism, defines our achievement society. "A purely hectic rush produces nothing new," Han writes. "It merely reproduces and accelerates what is already available."[14] Han cites Horkheimer and Adorno's colleague, Walter Benjamin, who proposed that forms of so-called boredom—listening deeply, without distraction, to a piece of music, or the world going by—could be a source of the new. Yet Han argues such inspiration is inaccessible to the contemporary mind, which is hyperactive: boredom is elusive and unthinkable to it.[15]

In one of *Dialectic of Enlightenment*'s most remarkable passages, Horkheimer and Adorno describe the section of the Ancient Greek poet Homer's the *Odyssey* in which Odysseus and his men encounter the Sirens. Odysseus, the Greek hero who makes his way home to Ithaca after the Trojan War, has suffered greatly, in combat and in journey. He looks perpetually to the future, where he will be reunited with his estate, which includes his wife, Penelope. He must turn away from the past, because dwelling on it too much would threaten his present drive to return home and thus his very survival.

For Horkheimer and Adorno, Odysseus's past represents Western humanity's own, which, if grasped, could derail the industrial self altogether. This past is not a vision of humanist reconstitution, a hippie utopia of nature, beauty, and reconnection. In Homer's poem, Odysseus's own recent past involves the violence of war, including, of course, killing by his own hand, and complete stasis, including being a prisoner of the flesh-eating cyclops Polyphemus and in sexual subjection to the witch Circe.

The Sirens sing a song that, if heard, lures any sailor to their death. The song pre-dates the culture industry and utterly opposes it, an intoxicating rest from the concepts of self, productivity, information, and use that Western culture upholds. The song calls for such total abandonment of ego that it demands death. Without some measure of control, the song will prevent Odysseus from returning home. But the song is not useless. It has one purpose only: to ecstatically kill Odysseus, his men, and anyone else who hears it.

Odysseus's brilliant idea is to listen, consequence-free. He harnesses the song like fossil fuel, along class lines—plugging his men's ears with wax and bidding them to row, hard. Whereas Odysseus means to deprive his workers entirely of the song—he needs their manpower to stay afloat, so they must not have it—he has different plans for himself. He asks his men to bind him to the mast of the ship so that he may listen to the Sirens without perishing. He may call out to his men for release, but they won't hear him. He's made sure of it.

"The epic already contains the correct theory," Horkheimer and Adorno write, comparing Odysseus to the applauding bourgeois concert goer of their time. "Between the cultural heritage and enforced work there is a precise correlation, and both are founded on the inescapable compulsion toward the social control of nature."[16]

* * *

One cannot refuse culture, however industrial it has become. As the British pop star Samantha Fox wrote in a 1986 review of the single "Panic" by the post-punk band The Smiths, for the music magazine *Smash Hits*, the same year she had her own smash hit with "Touch Me (I Want Your Body)":

I'm sorry to say but I find [The Smiths] very depressing. The lead singer's voice sounds like he's in pain—is that Morrissey? It says in the song "hang the DJ"—but where would they be without them? If you don't like DJs, you still *like* them because they play your records and that's what sells records... I wouldn't play [the record], though—he can't sing and it gives me a headache. In all his interviews he's Mister Nasty too and goes moan moan moan.[17]

Fox's observations again evoke Benjamin, whom Adorno had criticized for his "wide-eyed presentation of actualities"[18]—his love of trash. Just as Fox's practical acknowledgment of the material needs of the record industry cannot be separated from her disdain for The Smiths, and her desire to hear music that is not depressing, so Benjamin's attitude toward the culture industry as expressed in his 1935 essay "The Work of Art in the Age of Mechanical Reproduction" combines excitement with dismay.

In the Preface to his essay, Benjamin invokes the so-called dialectical materialism of Marx, which, like Hegel, considers two seeming opposites but, *contra* Hegel, does so for a material, not a conceptual, insight. This is typically a "demystification"—the undoing of a capitalist myth. (A Marxist dialectic of globalization might contrast its promise of international unity with the inequities it causes.) Within this dialectic, Benjamin considers the central ideas of traditional Marxism. First, that any given society has a "base," its economic underpinning, and a "superstructure," everything else, including culture, informed by this base. Second, that capitalism will eventually give way to socialist revolution, with the working class seizing control of the base. If there are signs of the working class seizing control of the base, Benjamin wonders, shouldn't this be noticeable in the superstructure, specifically in the culture industry? If so, might the culture industry be a tool for progressive change, a weapon against outdated, classist notions like "creativity and genius, eternal value and mystery," which were, in Benjamin's time, being glorified by various fascists?[19]

Art historians have tended to focus on a small section of Benjamin's essay: his description of the loss, in mechanical art, of essence or presence—the "aura."[20] This gives the false impression that Benjamin laments the absence of some important quality in mechanical art. Rather, Benjamin celebrates the loss of the aura as the loss of fixation on artistic purity. For the first time, mechanical art frees art of its ritualistic contexts. No longer is art hidden from the working class. Instead, Benjamin argues, mechanical art, widely available, begins to take on a political function.[21] Such art grants its audiences agency, exposing, not hiding, how art is made and behaves in the world. Such art is literally exhibitionist, wanting to be seen by as many people as possible, not secreted away like some relic.

The popular film, for instance, turns the audience into a critic, making them identify not with actors but with the camera, a machine whose function is, like all technology, to produce, test, and verify. Close-ups allow film audiences to be psychoanalysts, to appreciate the small twitches and quirks of human behaviour in a "mutual penetration of art and science."[22] Mechanical art such as a horror film may give audiences a shock, but this same audience will scoff at an avant-garde painting that also intends to shock, because the painting demands a different, older, ritualistic sort of attention. The distraction of a film is liberating. It gives audiences the option *not* to pay close attention and at the same time rewards any close attention paid.

Five years after "The Work of Art in the Age of Mechanical Reproduction," Benjamin overdosed on morphine while fleeing the Gestapo. In his essay's Epilogue, he revisits the fascist fixation on "creativity and genius, eternal value and mystery" from his Preface. It is not that the fascists reject mechanical art. Rather, they make mechanical art *into* ritual. They use the wide reach and compellability of mechanical art to make it *appear* as if working people are assuming control of the base. Fascist mechanical art gives audiences the unlimited capacity to express but does nothing to improve the conditions of their lives, promising everything and delivering nothing. Meanwhile, fascism glorifies war and destruction as the ultimate artwork. "The logical result of Fascism," Benjamin writes, "is the introduction of aesthetics into political life."[23]

* * *

What of the introduction of political life into aesthetics? The important work of Jamaican-British cultural-studies theorist, educator, and sociologist Stuart Hall[24] sits between Benjamin and Han, spanning the decline of the modern after World War II and the emergence of the postmodern and contemporary, notably the mid-1980s information revolution after which art, in the form of creativity and expression, became a default way of being.

Hall's sensible consideration of how the culture industry works reflects his peculiar generational position. Born only a few years before Benjamin's essay, and with the perspective of a middle-class racialized immigrant, Hall was too old to be a Baby Boomer but young enough to understand what it meant to be raised within and by the culture industry, to have its media and products shape and speak to him. For Hall, a lifelong leftist, there was no escaping a consideration of the popular and its economy of the new. To dismiss this was to dismiss groups of people for whom his politics advocated.

Hall was part of the British iteration of the so-called New Left, which spanned the late 1950s to the 1970s and aimed to make the left relevant again after its earlier failings and attendant stigmatization during the Cold War. Known for its cultural focus, the New Left provided a framework for social-justice movements to follow such as second-wave feminism, Black Power, gay liberation, and more. The standard old-school Marxist critique of the New Left was that the base could never be changed through the superstructure. Yet, the culture industry's influence had grown so much in the 1950s and 1960s that it seemed foolish to ignore it. Weaned on ever-intrusive TV and advertising, with the associated conviction that the personal was political, the New Left could not abandon the images and products that had been so formative to them. If the culture industry could raise them, could it not change other things? The emerging field of cultural studies was part of the gambit. Here, the director of a Hollywood film could be its author, and popular culture could be ironic and subversively funny—"camp." Popular culture was art, art was popular culture, and both, it seemed, could be political.

So it was that Hall wished to take the culture industry's fixations, including the new, seriously. Yet, he increasingly warned readers of the limits of its progressive uses. His 1964 book with Paddy Whannel, *The Popular Arts*, looked at the culture industry from the position of education, aiming to confront working-class students with the culture they so often used to resist their teachers. In the book, Hall and Whannel make a distinction between mass art—the culture industry at its trashiest—and popular art, which effectively comes from Williams's idea of folk art. Popular art was, for the authors, Miles Davis, mass art Liberace.[25] Popular art was the perverse, knowing sexuality of Hollywood film star Marlene Dietrich,[26] mass art the tabloid pin-up. Both forms of art can instruct, the authors argued. Mass art does so through its structure and sociological effect, popular art through its engaging content.

By the time Hall published the 1981 essay "Notes on Deconstructing 'The Popular,'" things had changed. Prime Minister Margaret Thatcher had seized populism in Britain in a manner that had shocked and destabilized the left. Thatcherism, a concept Hall had identified and developed, was, along with Reaganomics in the USA, prefiguring what has become known as neoliberalism, the all-encompassing ideology of our time in which no aspect of life escapes free-market interest. Even in Hall's time, neoliberalism was, its prefix notwithstanding, not new. Neoliberalism's intrusiveness and focus on nonstop work evoke Horkheimer and Adorno's culture industry. Its political deployment of media to capture voters, hype newness, and trumpet change evokes Benjamin's fascism—promising much and delivering, for most, very little.

In "Notes on Deconstructing 'The Popular,'" Hall questions the either–or polarities by which the left of his day had come to see the popular. On one hand, some leftists viewed "popular" as the culture industry that pacified and manipulated the masses. Hall rejects this understanding as condescending and thus "deeply unsocialist."[27] Other leftists understood "popular" to mean something like what he and Whannel, following Williams, had asserted back in the 1960s: a subcultural and more authentic alternative to the mainstream, with roots in pre-industrial folk culture. For Hall, this latter understanding, formerly his own, ignores the patently cyclical qualities of culture. It particularly ignores the inherent function of the culture industry, whose obsession with the new keeps it in constant flux, on purpose.

Hall concludes that the culture industry's true influence lies in its shifting nature—its expression of power and domination. The culture industry never grants full autonomy, was never meant to. At the same time, we are not blank slates upon which popular culture inscribes itself. Those who find recognition in the culture industry's products may also find power in them. They are engaged in something far too complex to be called pure coercion.[28]

For Hall as for Benjamin, popular culture raises the political stakes of cultural shifts, giving them a combative quality. The culture industry disorganizes, then reorganizes and shapes, expression to fit dominant forms. Culture, with or without industry, always keeps going, with characteristic uncertainty. Within industry, consumers identify with and recognize themselves in products and also resist their dominant messaging. This resistance stops, however, when consumers mistake such products as whole, coherent, stable—either totally authentic or totally corrupt—and, whatever their cast, here to stay.[29]

Before today's culture wars, Hall had a more general understanding of culture itself as a war for value—what it is, and how it's made. For Hall, culture's true war has no end. Rather, things, in Hall's words, "go up the cultural escalator"[30] and then must go back down. The literal currency of culture is made up of what is sacred and profane: in Nietzsche's words, the Apollonian (after the Greek god of knowledge and light) and the Dionysian (after the Greek god of wine and madness),[31] or, in French singer-songwriter Serge Gainsbourg's words, "*qui est 'in'*" and "*qui est 'out.*'"[32] To be politically empowered by the culture industry, audiences must be aware of its perpetual practice of dethroning and anointing—and proceed with caution.

Hall's ideas are unmistakably influenced by the Italian Marxist philosopher Antonio Gramsci, who was imprisoned by his country's fascist government in the 1920s, with the bulk of Gramsci's work, now known as *The Prison Notebooks*, not published until the late 1940s. At present, Gramsci is best known for his concept of hegemony, a term that itself has gone up the cultural escalator and back down. Now shorthand for any apparently dominant ideology, Gramsci's original idea of hegemony considers how power comes to *appear* natural, via the "common sense" of the dominant forces of any given society.[33]

In the 1960s and 1970s, the New Left saw Gramsci as an appealing figure because he believed in resistance through the superstructure—including, especially, culture. Largely from middle-class and upper middle-class families, the New Left was increasingly uninterested in Gramsci's anti-utopianism, and instead emphasized culture as a site of radical change. For Gramsci, however, change was always an uncertain process, and not a singular or permanent event. His theory of a so-called counterhegemonic bloc, in which the dominated classes push back against common sense—with "good sense"—is not guaranteed or inevitable.[34] Indeed, there are many instances in which good sense quickly *becomes* common sense—aided, indispensably, by the culture industry. Consider Tom Wolfe's 1970 essay "These Radical Chic Evenings," a tart portrait of a cocktail party hosted by US conductor Leonard Bernstein at his Park Avenue duplex in Manhattan, at which white liberal celebrities hobnobbed with members of the Black Panthers.[35] In Wolfe's contentious view, all guests at the Bernsteins were united in their efforts to assert and strengthen their cultural currency. Real, practical change was, Wolfe implied, an afterthought.

Gramsci's work informs the cultural studies field and its subsets, media studies and media literacy, educational areas for which Hall tirelessly advocated. Media literacy urges a critical stance toward the culture industry and its media, encouraging students to be different kinds of critics than the distracted ones Benjamin had identified. Such literacy makes an ever-unfashionable request: to see outside the culture industry's power in consideration of a different kind of power—analytical observation. It does not ask for complete disengagement, which it knows, in a hyper-mediated time, is impossible. Rather, as Hall noted again and again, media literacy tries to accept the culture industry for what it is, lest it become all there is.

* * *

The 1980s were to see a moral panic about rap and heavy metal music, which Hall foresaw in his own writings about race, class, and crime. This panic viewed the consumption of media as, in Hall's words, "behavioural input, like a tap on the kneecap."[36] The panic came precisely from the conviction that the culture industry could have a lasting effect on social conditions—a central tenet of New Left thought.

Radical-left protest of the 1980s continued to use culture as a political instrument. The US-based demonstrations of AIDS Coalition to Unleash Power (ACT UP) used avant-garde aesthetics, the shock of a certain kind of new, to raise awareness and call for policy reform. By the time the Irish singer-songwriter Sinead O'Connor did an acapella version of Bob Marley and the Wailers's "War" on a 1992 episode of *Saturday Night Live*, a late-night comedy-sketch show on a major TV network (NBC), activist performance art had gone mainstream. O'Connor's choice of "War," Marley's adaptation of an address given by Ethiopian emperor and Rastafari icon Haile Selassie to the United Nations in 1963, was apposite. Before concluding by ripping up a picture of Pope John Paul II to protest the Catholic Church's record of child abuse, O'Connor pointedly sang the song's urging: until humanity had achieved universal equality, "everywhere is war."[37] Among the battlegrounds was, as her own performance made clear, all aspects of culture, above all its far-reaching industry.

For Hall, the popularization of politics-as-culture, and vice versa, was a tenet of Thatcherism. By 1987, Thatcher had won her third election in Britain, and Hall wrote of Thatcherism as a full-on ideology that exploited "the fears, the anxieties, the lost identities, of a people."[38] Thatcherism rendered politics in images. It addressed collective fantasies and smothered leftist talk of the day, which had become mired in dry academese. Also in 1987: Thatcher gave a notorious interview to *Woman's Own* magazine, in which she claimed there was "no such thing" as society, only component individuals who "look to themselves first."[39] It is worth repeating that Thatcherism was a political version of Horkheimer and Adorno's culture industry: mass engagement predicated on individual, alienated consumption. After Thatcher, any successful politician, no matter how progressive, would have to capture hearts and minds through this industry. (While O'Connor sang on

Saturday Night Live, US Democrat Bill Clinton was running a successful presidential campaign marked by sax solos on the *Arsenio Hall Show* and Baby Boomer pop-rock band Fleetwood Mac's "Don't Stop" as his campaign theme.)

Hall never lost his faith in the sophistication of audiences. His 1980 essay "Encoding/Decoding" resists decades-old, post-World War II government- and corporate-funded research that saw the modern media as a conduit for the global spread of liberalism.[40] Such research used scientific methodology to claim that media might function as that "tap on the kneecap," where TV and radio programs communicated preconceived messages, sent directly to receptive audiences in a kind of closed, efficient, propagandistic circuit.

Neither Hall nor Thatcher believed culture worked that way. For Hall, any reception of media is part of the practical, real-life moments during which it is delivered, and on which it is based. Any given moment can throw the intended meaning of a media product into question. Producers who realize this shape their content accordingly, into stories—making the audience both source and receiver of the message.[41] The story comes *from* the audience and is given back *to* them, to be re-made anew: encoded. This possibility of communicative feedback is built into the form of many media products. Producers cannot predict all new phenomena that might arise in the process—which may prompt *decoding*, a form of distortion and potential resistance.

For Hall, there are three main approaches to decoding. The first is dominant-hegemonic: an audience member takes the message straight and decodes it according to its encoding, which may involve the media source trying its best not to show any bias or intolerance. The second is negotiated code: an audience member acknowledges the dominant-hegemonic encoding but decodes within their own situation or circumstance. Negotiated code is "in one ear and out the other": the decoder properly decodes but may feel the message has no relation to their own life, or decides, for whatever reason, that it is not worth considering. The third is when the audience member truly understands the encoded message, but decodes it in a contrary manner, deconstructing, then reconstructing, within "some alternative framework of reference."[42]

Hall's description feels nostalgic in the digital era, where there seems no dominant culture, and boundaries between producer, audience, and product are utterly indistinct. Users create content, appearing to exert unprecedented control over encoding. But they are subject to incessant, refracted corporate decodings. Social-media companies are the new mass audiences, watching users, their data-mining industry captive not just to user content but also to moment-by-moment user behaviour. Hall's media-literate decoder has morphed into these sophisticated, aligned companies. Tech giants are also Benjamin's critic-audience, their media-literate tools scrutinizing users-as-product to determine the best way to decode. Users' acts of expression, opinion, or observation become various dependencies—collective patterns of use put up for sale.

As encoded and decoded products, users complicate any determinedly critical response from other users. The sheer volume of work requires the hypervigilance of which Han speaks and is managerial, not negotiated. A user's own options for decoding are, unlike those of digital corporations, limited, antisocial: deleting, self-silencing, disconnecting, disguising.

German sociologist Andreas Reckwitz critiques a contemporary society infatuated with art and creativity, noting that it is not just ruthless, evil capitalism that has swooped in to conquer aesthetics. Rather, cultural and economic interests are entwined. The culture industry may not be a rising tide that lifts all boats, but it is relentless, making constant value from valuelessness, and vice versa. It has other commercial attractions. Digital culture's particular devotion to creativity and expression may be the latest placeholder for religion, myth. Reckwitz argues that, within neoliberalism, with its boom-and-bust, crisis-oriented cycles, people struggle to find motivation to participate as workers, spenders, investors. Enter culture, everywhere. For Reckwitz, *homo aestheticus* has become *homo economicus*'s best friend.[43]

One should not underestimate culture; one should not overestimate it either. Philosophical jurisprudence presents the Critical Legal Theorists as figures, some former lawyers, who became disenchanted after Civil Rights cases such as *Brown v. Board of Education* seemed neither to greatly alter the judiciary's attentiveness to inequity nor to beat a clear path to law reform. Like much of academia in the 1970s, the Critical Legal Theorists turned to post-structuralist theory for guidance. Yet, the judicial branch of most democratic governments, like the culture industry (and any language system), is designed as a site of interpretation and contestation, not as an engine of reform—something of which the judiciary, in many cases appointed, not elected, must be careful, or risk overstepping their role.

Despite this, since the 1970s, there has been an increased reliance on Western court systems to grant justice that legislation often refuses. Left-liberal Supreme Court judges stress the importance of their own progressive rulings, but these rulings exist in newly tentative spaces, waiting to be affirmed or overruled, indeed, to become law. At the tipping point of universal suffrage in the 1970s, could it be that democratic systems revealed themselves as so plainly dysfunctional that people's attention turned from voting and protest to the courts, which were expected to provide reforms they were never designed to? Has the same happened with culture?

Like all cultural criticism, this is a theory and cannot be objectively verified.

2
Natural Supernatural

Life is strange
We hate to change from what is tried and true
Though I know I'm only doing what the others do
Still it all seems new.

—"Ev'rything's Been Done Before," a 1930s US song by Harry Adamson, Edwin Knopf, and Jack King, popularized by Al Bowlly and later by Louis Armstrong

Italian poet and philosopher Giacomo Leopardi's 1824 text *Dialogue between Fashion and Death* has Fashion and Death encountering each other in satirical debate. Fashion, purveyor of all things instantly, ephemerally new, insists she is Death's sister. Death doesn't believe her until she outlines the tortures, assimilations, distortions, and obliterations she can cause, then threatens Death that she will stop "the practice of dying," thus making what he does unfashionable.[1] Death accepts the siblinghood.

As Death struggles to see himself in Fashion, so contemporary culture, fixated on promises of change, struggles to see in its new things, or rather remember in them, the same. In a now famous image from his 1940 essay "Theses on the Philosophy of History," Benjamin conjures the *Angelus Novus* of avant-garde painter Paul Klee, seeing in Klee's work the "angel of history" getting blown by a storm into the future, his back turned from this forward direction, his face gazing at the debris history leaves behind. "This storm is what we call progress," Benjamin writes.² In his 1970 book *Aesthetic Theory*, Adorno presents the image of a child trying to play a never-before-heard chord on the piano. "The chord, however, was always there," Adorno writes. "The new is the longing for the new, not the new itself."³ In another dialogue with Hegel, Adorno suggests that, if the new in art attained any utopia, it would be art's end. For instance, if an architectural movement based on fantasy and whimsy permanently supplanted functionalism, this fantasy and whimsy would fast become kitsch, then a sort of endless torture. It is worth remembering that, in the 16th century, British philosopher Thomas More contrived the word utopia as a phonetic pun on a two-word Greek phrase, one meaning of which is "good place," the other "no place."⁴

Western culture's anti-utopianist figure, the dandy, emerged from 19th-century aestheticism and decadence as an early avant-garde symbol of refusal. He has long been the social stereotype of the gay male. The dandy turned from art's bourgeois utility, rejecting its functional deployment as a sentimental and moralistic diversion. Instead, he embraced uselessness, fickleness, fakery—which, holds the dandy, is all art is. In the 20th century, the dandy was employed as the culture-industry labourer *par excellence*: the designer, the dresser. In the 2019 film *Velvet Buzzsaw*, he is the bisexual art critic Morf Vandewalt (Jake Gyllenhaal), killed by the AI robot from Art Basel to whom he gives a bad review. Vandewalt's death is a choking from behind, unsurprisingly eroticized. A fetishist of the new in its cruellest forms, Vandewalt dies as he has lived.

In the introduction to his 2013 study *Novelty: A History of the New*, author Michael North details why what he is about to do feels not just redundant but confounding. In English there is not even a sufficient word for his topic. The word "newness" is awkward and fussy in usage. As an adjective, "novel" has a pejorative quality.[5] As a noun, of course, it means a book with a fictional narrative. In *The Novel: A Biography*, Michael Schmidt writes that "novel," up to the 18th century, meant something new, as well as a piece of news.[6] The English word "novel" is rooted in a utilitarian view of how fiction should be: new, and realist—like the news. The French and German word *roman* suggests a backward-looking form, that is, back to Roman times—artful, escapist. Schmidt theorizes that here is the difference between English pragmatism and continental-romantic sensibility.

The noun "novelty" is, for North, fully "shady," associated with the many consumer products of the modern period of the first half of the 20th century, and so connotatively antiquated.[7] This sense of remove—pure novelties (gadgets, trinkets, gewgaws, etc.) must be from a time different than our own—is telling. North points to a 1990s marketing firm that had determined that newness for newness's sake no longer had consumer cachet, and then to the art and fashion worlds, whose relationship with the new, at least after the 1960s, had not been wide-eyed and essentialist, but either entirely indifferent or hyper-knowing.[8] However, North writes, a desire for and interest in the new stubbornly persists. Here we go again, for the first time.

Expertise on the new is hardly limited to gay men, although it is a conspicuous facet of the history of white male thought. Because the new in Western culture is so elusive, those who claim to understand it tend to have serious ambition, presenting as strongmen able to dissect the new, precisely because they are immune from desiring it. North asserts that anything written about the new as a concept must, for instance, entail multidisciplinary theoretical knowledge, a combination of science, aesthetics, philosophy, economics, and perhaps linguistics and biology as well. Even the most well-known theories of the new on the academic left, those of French writers Gilles Deleuze and Felix Guattari, for instance, deploy extreme figurative language in discussing the concept: mutation, schizophrenia, torture, inhumanity. (In the mid-2000s, British-Israeli architect Eyal Weizman uncovered that Israeli Defence Forces had been using the ideas of Deleuze and Guattari, as well as those of French Situationist Guy Debord and the US artist Gordon Matta-Clark, to inform their actions on Palestinian villages.[9]) There is, North writes, a double bind in trying to define the new in culture, because it bears close resemblance to things culture is often perceived either to have little to do with or to reject outright, from empirical examination to economic theory. At the start of his influential 1974 study, *Theory of the Avant-Garde*, German critic Peter Bürger insists that what he is about to do should be called "critical literary science," something that seems to mean everything and nothing at once.[10]

In her 2014 piece "Delusions of Whiteness in the Avant-Garde," Cathy Park Hong looks on Bürger and his legacy, writing that "to argue what is and is not truly avant-garde now, based on say, Peter Bürger's definition of the avant-garde, would be a mind-numbing, self-defeating, and masturbatory exegesis."[11] It is hard to disagree. Park Hong decides that her definition of "avant-garde" is whatever the contemporary institution has canonized as such. So it is, perhaps, with the new, a concept Bürger's critical literary science tries to separate from the avant-garde. Still, like the avant-garde, the new, to use North's phrase, "tends to evaporate almost at the very instant it is recognized."[12] New things, whatever they are, *do* exist, and *can* be defined, but only by virtue of the less new things they make obsolete. This is both an economic and a behavioural understanding, not an intrinsic or formal one. Back to Adorno: the most illuminating history of the new in Western culture is not what it is or has been, but what the desire for and perception of it indicate. The West's history of the new is fraught with tension between isolation and collectivity, independence and dependence, value and worthlessness.

The basic conceptual models of the Western new have not, North argues, changed much since Plato.[13] Of course, the new is central to Western philosophy, including its meditations on time, change, free will, epistemology (ways of knowing), and ontology (ways of being). Yet, Western philosophy has only really determined two discernible types of new, which are self-debunking. First, the phenomenon of recurrence produces the *relatively* new: recurrence is prevalent in nature but does not offer the kind of pure novelty the Western imagination craves. Second, recombination *seems* to produce the new but only if we are to define the new in a half-new way: the "unprecedented relations between existing elements"[14] that are seen in music, mathematics, and language. Both types of new make pure novelty unreasonable and arbitrary, at worst meaningless. Nonetheless, in culture, this concept of pure novelty, never a technical-philosophical reality, bestows great value.

Postmodern and poststructuralist theory, now over half a century old, have done complex work trying to debunk and unravel the new and its functions. In the 1990s, the normalization of such theory seemed to suggest the advent of a more sophisticated, sobering perspective on the Western new. But theory's own proliferation and circulation in the academy turned it into an industry with a persistent craving for novelty. In his 2003 book *After Theory*, scholar Terry Eagleton waxes nostalgic about the 1960s and 1970s era of early postmodern theory. Then, Eagleton writes, theory was interdisciplinary, daringly prolific, a "library cataloguer's nightmare,"[15] and thus beyond the archive, the academy, the limits of then-current thinking. It was, he effectively argues, conceptually and methodologically new.[16] Now that the contemporary university has thoroughly embraced theory, it is in a bind. Graduate students and professors anxiously search for ever-niche contributions to their fields to gain ever rare professional footholds. The resource scarcity of the new that has long defined Western culture persists here. Vicious debates over who discovered or appropriated what—who owns what—have become the academy's latest obsession.

Back again to Adorno: the desire for and perception of the new is inherently melancholy. North observes that this is because, as an impossibility, the new is effectively an unfulfilled promise.[17] If the new cannot be truly found or otherwise held and sustained, it may lead to dissatisfaction, and so to suffering. Put another way, if a striving for the new, the original, results, as postmodernism suggests, only in difference, yet the promise of and faith in the new persists, feelings of stress and displacement are inevitable.[18]

In North's reading of Adorno, consumerism appears, anxiously, to manage this melancholy encounter with the new. In the West, the new is "on offer but never actually available,"[19] at once canceling itself out and creating demand, its inherent elusiveness simply making consumers want it more. The contemporary music industry is an accelerated example: fans hound artists for new material if more than a year passes without an album release. Then, if a release happens, and is well-received, threads populate with fans already saying they can't wait for the next one—an irritating kind of compliment. US pop artist Rihanna, who as of writing has not released an album since 2016, has turned such pressures into a kind of durational performance art. Her 2023 Superbowl halftime show, a medley of greatest hits, was the rare, stunning appearance of a withholding queen.

What does the new promise exactly? Western fine-art history suggests something nebulous and contradictory: the beautiful, made useful and good. The Roman encyclopedist Pliny the Elder characterizes the Greek artist Apelles of Kos as a type of elite athlete or businessperson. Apelles is better than any painter before or after him. When Apelles meets an elder painter in a line-drawing contest and wins, the results of the competition, where each draws lines on the same board, become an instructive artwork. Apelles is a sedulous practiser and draws every day, putting his drawings on a balcony and then hiding inside to listen to critiques from passers-by, to learn how to make his work better. Apelles uses an economy of materials to maximum effect, and seems to paint the unpaintable, his painted horses causing real horses to neigh in recognition. "All have profited by [Apelles'] innovations," Pliny writes, although none of these can be imitated.[20]

Almost 1500 years later, the Florentine artist Benvenuto Cellini wrote in his *Autobiography* about showing a just-finished sculpture of Jupiter to King Francis I. The problem: Cellini's rival Francesco Primaticcio had placed Cellini's sculpture in a roomful of bronze copies of Roman antiquities in an attempt to erase and sabotage Cellini's accomplishment. In a fairy-tale twist, the king's appreciation of Cellini's new creation directly turns on its placement among the old works. "Whoever it was wanted to do this man a bad turn," says the king, "has done him a great favour: the comparison with these splendid works of art only serves to make it apparent that his is more impressive and beautiful."[21]

In his 1963 essay "Norm and Form: The Stylistic Categories of Art History and their Origins in Renaissance Ideals," the Austrian art historian E.H. Gombrich writes that the sequential periods and styles of the Western art canon, with which everyone who attempts a study of the topic is still, however skeptically, familiar, "represents only a series of masks for two categories, the classical and the non-classical."[22] Gombrich does not mean to uphold the classical. He begins with the Italian Renaissance writer Giorgio Vasari's distaste for the Gothic style, which Vasari associates with "the hordes who destroyed the Roman Empire."²³ Gombrich finds the origins of Vasari's distaste in a Roman text by Vitruvius, *On Architecture* (27 BCE), in which Vitruvius denounces what he sees as the licentiousness and illogic in the decorative style that was fashionable in his time. Vitruvius writes:

> On the stucco are monsters rather than definite representations taken from definite things. Instead of columns there rise up stalks; instead of gables, striped panels with curled leaves and volutes. Candelabra uphold pictured shrines and above the summits of these, clusters of thin stalks rise from their roots in tendrils with little figures seated upon them at random. Again, slender stalks with heads of men and animals attached to half the body.
>
> Such things neither are, nor can be, nor have been. On these lines the new fashions compel bad judges to condemn good craftsmanship for dullness. For how can a reed actually sustain a roof, or a candelabrum the ornaments of a gable, or a soft and slender stalk a seated statue, or how can flowers and half-statues rise alternatively from roots and stalks? Yet when people view these falsehoods, they approve rather than condemn.²⁴

This is not just Vitruvius's personal distaste for the florid. Gombrich argues that the source of Vasari's anti-Gothic sentiments is the gold standard of Western design, the "hidden norm" of classicism, defined by Vitruvius as a kind of perfection, based on rule, order, measure, drawing, and style.²⁵ It is possible that every so-called movement in Western art history is not an innovation but a measure of compliance to this standard, the classical, and that whatever doesn't belong to this category falls into the loaded categories of the either not-yet-classical ("the barbaric") or the no-longer-classical ("the degenerate"). Gombrich's theory does not necessarily mean that anything not classical is permanently marginalized. Rather, this hidden norm creates a pendulum for the new to be constantly, if only seemingly, refreshed. For Gombrich, "the terminology of art history was... largely built on words denoting some principle of exclusion."[26] Here is one of many theories of the new as rooted, in a grasp for concrete existence, in the creation of taboos, others. While it purports to be creating, Western culture constantly manages.

Although Gombrich does not politicize his concept of exclusion, its imperialist, classist implications are clear, especially when he describes how the classical norm was instrumentalized beyond Italy. Celebrating Vasari's catholic approach to aesthetics, Gombrich writes, in contrast, that Northern Europe turned it into "inflexible dogma,"

> used by critics across the Alps who wanted to pit the classic ideals of perfection against local traditions. Gothic then became synonymous with that bad taste that had ruled in the Dark Ages, before the light of the new style was carried from Italy to the north.[27]

And so, the "new fashions" of which Vitruvius writes are an origin of kitsch, a concept of the new that, as we will see, offends established taste both by being too natural or folksy, and by being too artificial or sentimental.

Gombrich's tongue-in-cheek diction—"the light of the new style"—suggests an affinity between Vitruvius's normative aesthetics and Christianity. But isn't Vitruvius Christ's opposite—the former's pagan Roman Empire having killed Christ? Apparent opposites find strange alliances where the cultural new is concerned.

Before Christ, the idea that nothing comes from nothing—*ex nihilo nihil fit*—appears both in the thinking of pre-Socratic philosopher Parmenides, and in the Old Testament. Indeed, no study of the Western new would be complete without a nod to Ecclesiastes 1:9–10, which simply echoes the West's secular philosophical tradition:

> The thing that hath been, it is that which shall be; and that which is done is that which shall be done: and there is no new thing under the sun. Is there any thing whereof it may be said, See, this is new? It hath been already of old time, which was before us.[28]

Indeed, in *Novelty*, North puts this passage from Ecclesiastes in a trajectory that includes Parmenides and ends with Austrian philosopher Ludwig Wittgenstein, whose austere statement in the *Tractatus Logico-Philosophicus* seems to function as the last word on the topic: "If things can occur in states of affairs, this possibility must be in them from the beginning."[29] There is a resignation in Wittgenstein that feels very modern, like Adorno, and like Adorno's contemporary successors Han and Fisher. The new's last word in the West is, inevitably, the consequence of the West's misguided fixation: unglamorous reality, that is, unvarnished nature, revealed.

In the New Testament Gospels, Christ philosophizes about the new only once, in the Gospel of Matthew's parable of the garments and the wineskins. He says:

> No man putteth a piece of new cloth unto an old garment, for that which is put in to fill it up taketh from the garment, and the rent [i.e. tear] is made worse. Neither do men put new wine into old bottles: else the bottles break, and the wine runneth out, and the bottles perish: but they put new wine into new bottles, and both are preserved.[30]

The analogy, relevant to Christ's relationship to traditional Jewish law, suggests how the new doesn't fit with the old, setting the stage for Christ's revisionist teachings. Yet, the analogy also encourages slowness in the introduction of unfamiliar ideas. A new, unwashed cloth put on an old garment will shrink with washing and tear from that garment; new wine put in an old wineskin will ferment and stretch out that wineskin. Forcing the new on the old too quickly results in destruction, not growth.

After Christ's death, radical, spiritual truth merges with the new. Fraught with its usual contradictions, the new becomes a means by which to enter heaven, with mentions of the new increasing. Here is the story of the founding of the Christian church, effectively written by Paul the Apostle, who, in the book of Acts and under his Jewish name Saul, is struck down by a flash of light on the road to Damascus to become the world's first born-again Christian. From Acts until the last book of the Bible, Revelations, the new is no longer slow but fast, supernatural. In Acts 17:18, Paul, preaching the gospel, captivates the Epicureans and Stoics in Athens through their interest in new ideas. As atomist pagans, these Athenians would be a tough crowd, firm *ex nihilo nihil fit*–ites. Yet, when Paul begins writing to his missionaries in the Epistles, books falling between Acts and Revelations, he uses the model of Christ's birth, baptism, and raising from the dead to define the early Christian convert as born once more. This creation is not out of nothing; its strange logic suggests a return to a cleansed state that might be better than Eden.

To be born again in Pauline Christianity is to be regressively progressive. In II Corinthians 5:17, Paul writes, "Therefore if any man be in Christ, he is a new creature: old things are passed away; behold, all things are become new."[31] There is no precedent for Paul but Christ, who covers all. Paul writes in Colossians 3:9–11:

> Lie not one to another, seeing that ye have put off the old man with his deeds; And have put on the new man, which is renewed in knowledge after the image of him that created him. Where there is neither Greek nor Jew, circumcision nor uncircumcision, Barbarian, Scythian, bond nor free: but Christ is all, and in all.[32]

Paul's words resonate with contemporary globalization: integration and networking for the greater good. Unsurprisingly, by Revelations, the New Testament's language of the new takes on the tone of the nation-state, its new heaven, new earth, and New Jerusalem modelled after empire. North writes that the USA's founding fathers put *novus ordo saeclorum* (a new order of the ages) on the USA's Great Seal,[33] and then cites Arendt's observation in *On Revolution* that both the American and French Revolutions were not, according to many of their leaders, about moving forward but moving back. Specifically, they were about *restoring* an earlier period in which the so-called revolutionaries such as Thomas Paine believed they had possessed "rights and liberties of which tyranny and conquest had dispossessed them."[34]

As North notes, Pauline Christianity's ideological newness is the exact opposite of what Western philosophy concluded, initially, finally, and over and over.[35] In the place of *ex nihilo nihil fit*, Pauline Christianity posited *creatio ex nihilo*, the belief that God created the world out of nothing. *Creatio ex nihilo* was established as church dogma by the Fourth Lateran Council in 1215 but was taught well before then, an established idea even in the Christian philosopher Augustine's day.[36] Centuries after the Fourth Lateran Council, in Book VII of *Paradise Lost*, the British poet John Milton, a rationalist, anti-Royalist, and anti-Catholic Puritan, defaults to a Platonic reading of creation: forms come from formlessness, not nothing. This is the account that Genesis itself gives, more or less.

The implications of the shift to Pauline Christianity appear obvious: to deflect attention from what has been and what is; to wash clean and purify; to manifest and militarize; to disembody; to defeminize, extoling the highest forms of knowing and being as virgin births; to turn from death while maintaining a fixation with it; and to manage anxieties accompanying this denial. *Creatio ex nihilo* is Christ, packaged. When, in Shakespeare, King Lear says to Cordelia, "nothing will come of nothing,"[37] he may be indirectly blaspheming, arrogantly unaware of his tragic fate. But he is also at the very beginning of a process of emptying out and getting to the truth, naming that which he has neglected to see, which has been hidden from him by monarchy and the church's use of *creatio ex nihilo* as a tool to perpetuate his own power. When, in his 1975 art-critical study *The Painted Word*, Tom Wolfe writes, "first you get the word, then you can see,"[38] he is both mocking the theoretical justifications surrounding Abstract Expressionist painting and quoting the first line of the Gospel of John—placing the art world and indeed any culture industry in a similar category.

* * *

A cursory look at the cult that has formed around creativity, not just in the humanities but also in business and the science, technology, engineering, and mathematics (STEM) fields, confirms that *creatio ex nihilo* has not vanished as a value. Rather, it is in neoliberal duel with *ex nihilo nihil fit*. Creativity may seem to come out of thin air, but that must not, its proponents hold, be rationally true, and so there must be a way to determine its nature, and thus to harness it.

In his best-selling books, among them 2005's *Blink*, about the power of intuition, Canadian author Malcolm Gladwell matches the creative with the new. "It doesn't seem like we have much control over whatever bubbles to the surface from our unconscious," Gladwell writes. "But we do, and if we can control the environment in which rapid cognition takes place, then we can control rapid cognition."[39] Gladwell points to the renowned former director of New York's Metropolitan Museum of Art, Thomas Pearsall Field Hoving, who used to ask an assistant or fellow curator to hide whatever new thing the museum was considering acquiring in an unexpected place, like a coat closet. On eventually finding the thing, Hoving would "either feel good about it or suddenly… see something I hadn't noticed before."[40]

Quantifying and bottling creativity became a hallmark of the 2000s and 2010s. Blurbed by Gladwell, David W. Galenson's 2006 book, *Old Masters and Young Geniuses: The Two Life Cycles of Artistic Creativity*, divides famous artists into two categories: conceptual innovators, those who find success early in life by making sudden breakthroughs, and experimental innovators, those who work by trial and error to find success later in life.[41] Maria Popova, founder of *Brain Pickings*, a quirky literary blog popular in the 2010s, aligns her project with the philosophical new, but removes the skepticism:

> The core ethos… is that creativity is a combinatorial force: it's our ability to tap into our mental pool of resources—knowledge, insight, information, inspiration, and all the fragments populating our minds—that we've accumulated over the years just by being present and alive and awake to the world, and to combine them in extraordinary new ways. In order for us to truly create and contribute to the world, we have to be able to connect countless dots, to cross-pollinate ideas from a wealth of disciplines, to combine and recombine these pieces and build new ideas.[42]

In a resource-scarce world, creativity is construction, germination. A quote attributed to the US poet and novelist Maya

Angelou goes, "You can't use up creativity. The more you use, the more you have." Versions circulating online commonly gloss the quote with "creativity is a renewable resource,"[43] making the sentiment conspicuously extractive.

The prevalence of creativity as a value coincided with the prevalence of science as a value. The British authors Christopher Hitchens and Richard Dawkins updated modern secular philosophers such as Bertrand Russell for the post-9/11 era in their bestselling 2000s books *God Is Not Great* (Hitchens) and *The Selfish Gene* (Dawkins). Here, a liberal culture of positivism pitted itself against the religious fundamentalism that characterized the US neoconservative movement under President George W. Bush. Science was the antidote to organized religion and its dogmatic-doctrinal evils.

Like the economy, science has a tendency to present itself as the solution to its own problems—which in turn are presented as minor, necessary consequences of the progress science has granted. In 2014's *This Changes Everything: Capitalism vs. the Climate*, the Canadian author Naomi Klein paints a dreadful vision of a world under geo-engineering, a phenomenon in which technology saves humanity from global warming by altering the atmosphere, the ocean, and more, trapping carbon and life as we know it in the process. The spirit of geo-engineering is old. Klein cites the 17th-century British scientist, philosopher, and politician Francis Bacon, a key source of Western property law, whose 1623 *De Augmentis Scientiarum* reads:

> For you have but to follow and as it were hound nature in her wanderings, and you will be able, when you like, to lead and drive her afterwards to the same place again... Neither ought a man to make scruple of entering and penetrating into these holes and corners, when the inquisition of truth is his sole object.[44]

Bacon's gendered science-as-violence resonates centuries later in British writer Mary Shelley's novel *Frankenstein*, born of its author's nightmares and 1816's bad, cold summer, which, like the Ice Age, may have been caused by a volcanic explosion, the exact type of phenomenon geo-engineering tries to mimic. Naturally, *Frankenstein*'s ghost story is a warning about the converging of creativity and science, and the consequences of the inventor's unbounded ego.

North's own Bacon quote comes from *Novum Organum* (1620): "The true and lawful goal of the sciences is none other than this: that human life be endowed with new discoveries and powers."[45] This is a clear recasting of Pauline Christianity. Bacon was certainly a Christian, his paragon of the God-fearing scientist in evidence, as Hitchens notes in *God Is Not Great*,[46] in one of the epigraphs of Darwin's *On the Origin of Species*, an excerpt from Bacon's *Advancement of Learning*:

> Let no man out of a weak conceit of sobriety, or an ill-applied moderation, think or maintain, that a man can search too far or be too well studied in the book of God's word, or in the book of God's works; divinity or philosophy; but rather let men endeavor an endless progress or proficiency in both.[47]

"Man" the Enlightenment scientist is born again, as discoverer with endless bounds and powers, his rebirth making God more knowable. This is precisely the critical topic of Shelley's novel, a masterpiece of feminist Romanticism that delves into the possibilities and terrors of accelerated individualist thinking.

So it is that although culture may feel second fiddle to the STEM fields, there is, per Horkheimer and Adorno's critique of positivism, a fundamental link. Thomas Kuhn's 1962 best-selling book *The Structure of Scientific Revolutions* appears in

North's book as inevitably as it does here. Although Kuhn's book does not intend to be the last word on its subject of how scientific discoveries are made, it has introduced a term, "paradigm shift," into the cultural vernacular, the ossified meaning of which has only vague associations with its origins. Kuhn himself preferred "paradigm change."[48]

In his book, Kuhn portrays science both as mundane, hard work, and as a site of mystery and epiphany. This seductive image informs the neoliberal dream of individuals finding and making value anywhere, at any time, through constant work and experimentation—for the collective good. Kuhn's book provided another reason for contemporary culture to advocate for science alongside creativity, technology, and business. Indeed, Kuhn's vision of a labour force dedicated to invention has had lasting impact. The term "art world," for instance, can partly be attributed to Kuhn. The US critic-philosopher Arthur Danto wrote his essay "The Artworld" in 1964, at the height of the popularity of Kuhn's book. Danto's "artworld" was, he noted, conceptual, not a real place,[49] but later, in the 1974 essay "What is Art? An Institutional Analysis," US scholar George Dickie wrote of an actual, institutional "artworld,"[50] his theory also attributable to Kuhn's influence,[51] with "world" soon becoming insider shorthand for culture industry subsections under globalization—the film world, the music world, etc.

Kuhn's book is a critique of what he describes as the "development-by-accumulation"[52] theory of scientific discoveries. Kuhn is not directly calling into question the values and political deployments of science but rather an understanding of science that places inventors, singly and one after another, in a kind of relay race for ultimate knowledge, a history of science that bears resemblance to the history of fine art Gombrich scrutinizes. However, although Kuhn questions the linear storytelling of his field, he, like Gombrich, does not dispose of storytelling summarily. In Kuhn's perspective, the emerging self-awareness of science about what feels wrong (and right) in any given research narrative brings about the precise conditions—crisis—that lead to what he sees as actual change and invention, newness.

Instead of linearity Kuhn sees patterns: disciplinary, professional, arguably industrial. Kuhn uses "paradigm" to describe the shared aspects of professional communication in science that remain essentially unquestioned and allow for "the relative unanimity of professional judgments."[53] Simply put, Kuhn's paradigm is an agreed-upon style of thinking that dominates research. Eventually, the paradigm becomes destabilized, typically through an achievement that is unprecedented enough to attract a loyal and growing group of scientists away from competing activities, and that is open-ended enough to leave many and different types of problems for this group to explore and attempt to resolve. This is the revolution that is the subject of Kuhn's book.

Kuhn's idea of newness is unmistakably relational. It depends equally on conformists and renegades, the former much greater in number. Kuhn uses "normal science" to describe the activity of most scientists, practitioners whose labour is occasioned precisely because of the messiness of the revolutions.[54] These normal scientists try, in small, humble tasks, to refine the consequences of the shift. North describes Kuhn's normal scientists as "worker bees," who toil like the well-oiled parts of an intricately designed machine.[55] This vision of normal scientists working collectively, each in their own productive way, in pursuit of the refinement of an agreed-upon idea, suggests many ideological movements in religion, politics, and of course culture. "New" had already been a buzzword in the avant-garde and culture industry alike since modernism. Yet, Kuhn's scientific model gives an optimistic spin both to the Futurists and to Horkheimer and Adorno. Kuhn's was an economic theory for science that might just work to keep art relevant in the public eye, making what many felt to be a useless thing eminently useful: art as culture, culture as science, and everything as workshop.

However, Kuhn's theory does not readily apply to art. Art has an inherent emphasis not only on individuality but also on exceptionalism. North writes that Kuhn:

> continually quarrels with the Romantic view of scientific discovery as the work of particular individuals driven by quasi-divine inspiration. In a sense, then, the term *normal science* is redundant, or even misleading, if it is taken to imply that some other sort of science is possible. Normal science, science conducted within a paradigm with the intention of reinforcing and advancing its presuppositions, is the only kind of science there is.[56]

To wit, would any artist accept the self-description "normal artist"? In 1974, Dickie, a critic not an artist, wrote of the "people who keep the machinery of the artworld working and thereby provide for its continuing existence."[57] The contemporary creative economy is indeed full of its own types of worker bees: editors, curators, technicians, assistants, but also, yes, the majority of artists, whose primarily non-innovative contributions to any given paradigm reinforce dominant ideas and/or refine and interrogate them, what Kuhn called, within normal science, "mop-up work," and which he praised as fascinating.[58] In MFA programs, students and instructors alike are dedicated to such mop-up work, reminding each other of what is current in whatever media or field, and placing people and work within appropriate professional networks. Kuhn's description of the work of normal science includes determining a paradigm's significant facts, matching these facts with theory, and (re)articulating theory—the thrust not just of MFA programs but of most humanities academia, to say nothing of publishers, or art institutions.

Although Kuhn resists a Romantic view, his description of how revolution occurs has unquestionable glamour and mystification, making it attractive to our creativity-obsessed times. A paradigm shift will arise, like *kairos*, from crisis. Nature will persistently contradict the paradigm. There will be an attendant demand for paradigm destruction and thus a profound shift in the work of normal science.[59] The period preceding the destruction is one of insecurity, instability, failure. Such crisis is reminiscent of neoliberal economics, which famously see opportunity in instability. Yet, Kuhn's crisis is "a conversion experience that cannot be forced."[60] Rather, a Kuhnian revolution occurs by necessity because revolution is expensive, resource-wise: like the manufacturing industry, science can't afford the extravagant expense of radical change. "Paradigm shift" may now be bandied about by journalists describing every little cultural or political thing that shocks and surprises, but Kuhn was talking about something bigger. North compares Kuhn's revolution to Pauline conversion,[61] and Kuhn himself believed science's revolutions made it distinct "from every other creative pursuit except perhaps theology."[62]

What, in Kuhn, pushes crisis into paradigm shift? As North notes, switch-flicking arises from the frustrated work of normal science, a perspective shift like the image-analogies in Gestalt therapy, where a duck can suddenly become a rabbit, or a young woman an old lady, depending on how one encounters them. Kuhn writes of dreamtime illumination, inundation, lightning flashes, and scales falling from the eyes:

> The new paradigm... emerges all at once, sometimes in the middle of the night, in the mind of a man deeply immersed in crisis. What the nature of that final stage is... must here

remain inscrutable and may be permanently so. Let us here note only one thing about it. Almost always the men who achieve these fundamental inventions of a new paradigm have been either very young or very new to the field whose paradigm they change... [T]hese are the men who, being little committed by prior practice to the traditional rules of normal science, are particularly likely to see that those rules no longer define a playable game and to conceive another set that can replace them.[63]

The figure who can see the new is new themselves. As North observes, this figure may initially be seen as a fraud, their observations as mistakes, embarrassments—until they break through. The "conversion experience," in Kuhn's wording, "cannot be forced."[64]

Newness in the West has thrived precisely on the contradiction in Kuhn between pragmatism and epiphany. Kuhn's tale in *The Structure of Scientific Revolutions* recalls the passage in Said's *Orientalism* dealing with French novelist Gustav Flaubert's unfinished 1880 novel *Bouvard et Pécuchet*. In Said's interpretation of Flaubert's notes, the character Bouvard, who contends that, soon, "Europe will be regenerated by Asia," stands as a lampoon of secular, rationalist, post-Enlightenment Western thought, which reverts back to Christian notions of fate and destiny whenever it wants to maintain dominance, containment, control. Bouvard's "new, revitalized Europe" comes from classical Christian notions of death, followed by rebirth and redemption. Said uses US literary scholar M.H. Abrams's term "natural supernaturalism" to describe this post-Enlightenment religiosity.[65] Said writes,

> But it was not just any science [Flaubert] mocked: it was enthusiastic, even messianic European science, whose victories included failed revolutions, wars, oppression, and

an unteachable appetite for putting grand, bookish ideas quixotically to work immediately. What such science or knowledge never reckoned with was its own deeply ingrained and unself-conscious bad innocence and the resistance to it of reality... In short, such a scientist does not recognize in his science the egoistic will to power that feeds his endeavors and corrupts his ambitions.[66]

"Natural supernaturalism" could define liberal-secular arguments to Hitchens and beyond, including political commentator Andrew Sullivan's argument in a 2020 column for *New York* magazine's *Intelligencer* espousing liberalism as "not just a set of rules. There's a spirit to it."[67]

Kuhn's view of scientific revolution contains traces of mysticism. At the same time, like so many other Western writers on creativity, innovation, and the new, Kuhn strives to make these phenomena natural. North notes that although Kuhn makes scant mention of Darwin, an "intellectual version of a genetic mutation" is what he's after.[68] A theory of the new-as-industry can feel both Darwinian and Christian if it is an idea that is naturalized, presented as *simply the way things are*. "What might look to others like contradictions," North writes, citing how Kuhn's scientific innovation ultimately reinforces consistency in scientific practice, "actually occur in Kuhn's system as moments in a self-sustaining cycle and thus lose even the slim potential for change inherent in contradiction."[69]

If, as a worker in an innovation-seeking industry, I know that revolution could occur, but not how or when, but that this is nonetheless what I am tending to, my thoughts might take on a particular cast. I might, for instance, be humbler, trusting that I am part of some normal science, and that therefore what I do, even though it is creative, actually precisely because it is, can be acceptable and useful even if it is mundane. That what I do, if successful, is part of a paradigm, consensus, or conversation, which I must study and learn. That if I do not work within this paradigm, consensus, or conversation, I am being ignorant and arrogant (there is no other paradigm, not yet) and also giving up the possibility to contribute, because the only lasting creative contribution can be here. That even if I am part of normal science, I can feel confident, proud, that my work is strong enough to enliven this paradigm, consensus, or conversation. That I have been conscripted as a professional. That I am fit enough to contribute to this ecology. That my accomplishments are the result both of deliberation, and of the natural order of things.

At the same time, I might wonder: Am I the one? If I were, would I know? Certainly, my colleagues wouldn't. Humility and ego blur; inferiority and superiority complexes merge. If conversion takes time, how should a misunderstood prophet be? "Copernicanism made few converts for almost a century after Copernicus' death," Kuhn writes. "Newton's work was not generally accepted, particularly on the Continent, for more than half a century."[70] Kuhn quotes Darwin's *On the Origin of Species*:

> Although I am fully convinced of the truth of the views given in this volume... I by no means expect to convince experienced naturalists whose minds are stocked with a multitude of facts all viewed, during a long course of years, from a point of view directly opposite to mine... [B]ut I look with confidence to the future,—to young and rising naturalists, who will be able to view both sides of the question with impartiality.[71]

My field abides by unalterable rules that are natural—organic, alive, moving, changing—and also touched by mystery. I have little control over this nature or mystery. However, my faith is necessary. And although my work may be hard, this faith is easy to muster. Because in doing this, any, work, I am blessed. I am part of an industry. I am, perhaps, Said's bad innocent.

* * *

In his 1992 book *On the New*, the Russian theorist Boris Groys refers to what is translated from the German as "the well-known Van Gogh complex."[72] I can find little information on this complex or its psychopathology. The meaning is easy to infer, however. An artist is convinced they are misunderstood but that they must persist, tortured in their vision, because someone, somewhere, at some time, will appreciate their work. If the Van Gogh complex has fueled the culture industry, fostering countless vain hopes, debunking it has also become an industry.

In their 2018 *Netflix* special *Nanette*, the Australian comedian Hannah Gadsby relates the story of a man who tells them they should get off antidepressants because they're creative. "If Vincent van Gogh had taken medication, we wouldn't have *The Sunflowers*," the man tells them. Deploying their studies in art history, Gadsby rebuts: Van Gogh did in fact see psychiatrists and take medication, including foxglove, which may have caused him to see the colour yellow more vividly. "What do you honestly think?" asks Gadsby, exasperated. "That creativity means you must suffer? That [suffering] is the burden of creativity—just so you can enjoy it? Fuck you mate. If you like sunflowers so much, buy a bunch and go jerk off in a terrarium."[73]

For Hegel, even to discuss art's usefulness in philosophical or scientific terms was a morbid coming-after. In his lectures on aesthetics, Hegel defines art's proper "vocation" as revealing the truth by appealing to the senses.[74] He looks back fondly at the Ancient Greeks, who, in his view, worshipped truth and sensory form as one. He assesses medieval Christianity, in which, he observes, there were inklings of distance from the unadulterated veneration of material art. In his own time, Hegel laments that a type of scientific judgment rules art, which has died a kind of death, no longer living to be worshipped and thus, in its most essential form, a thing of the past.[75] In contemporary times, with art as Hegel saw it long dead, art's vocation is vocation itself—professionalism, accorded its own, special kind of worship.

Groys's book, originally written in Russian and published in German in 1992, then rewritten in German and published in English in 2014, reads almost like a post-Marxist *How to Succeed in Culture Without Really Trying*, except it offers no formula for success. Rather, Groys's book is bluntly amoral, a sequel to Nietzsche that, through dense theory, discloses an open secret about the new: the economy of Western culture shifts according to its own logic, with the topmost goal of keeping itself alive. There is no utopic endpoint to this culture, where nothing lasts forever. Here, the code of the new can only be described, never fully cracked.

For Groys, nothing is older or more conservative than a preoccupation with the new, which is based on compliance with Western culture's time-honoured rules of value.[76] Newness does not constitute one revelation after another, but one *revaluation* after another. Art is not about truth, but value—art's own lasting truth. The revaluation process of newness is in fact the only so-called truth in Western culture, which, from the Greeks onward, acknowledges that art cannot represent reality, only mimic and mediate it. Indeed, when ideas of pure truth or reality show up in Western art, they compromise art's value, its only acceptable currency—because such ideas suggest art is a mere lens or portal through which to get at truth.[77] After all, if art were only about access to truth, it would have served its purpose long ago.

That said, nothing seems truer to consumers of Western culture than a new work of art. New art can seem more authentic than reality itself. For Groys, the new is made when what has been considered "true" or "refined," that is, valuable, goes through a process of de-valuation, and what has been considered "profane, alien, primitive, or vulgar" becomes valuable.[78] The value of the new work is thus in how successfully it attains its newness, in relation. Something that is successfully new will aspire to the heights of tradition while at the same time be anathema to it. The cultural new is made by accurately seeing tradition and negatively adapting to it.

The Groysian new is importantly and utterly dependent on some kind of archive. No society will have an interest in innovation where there are no archives, and so the new can only come into being in a society with sufficient technical and social means of cultural preservation. Indeed, a society without an archive would risk its entire existence if it embraced the new. Tradition in the form of the archive is thus the basis of the new because the archive makes sure the new cannot endanger cultural memory. Rather, the new refreshes it, preserving tradition's very identity.

A culture of the new is not about a valued work attaining perpetual prominence. The archive makes a different kind of culture possible. In the shadow of the new, ambitious artists are concerned with being "unrepeatable for all time"—gaining perpetuity through originality, specificity, individuality.[79] It is in this way that an artist becomes new, which is a ticket to the archive. Such originality is not easy, however. Nor is it simply a matter of being different, or other. Rather, culture sees the new as not just any other but the *valuable* other: the other that seems to be in a process of breaking away from its so-called profane origins, enough to make it seem worthy of study, preservation, and criticism. Time merely passing cannot create such new things. They are dependent on social memory, never on individual discrimination. "The new is new only," Groys writes, "when it is new."[80]

Fashion, for Groys, is an impressive instance of the new at work. Those who dismiss fashion mistakenly believe that it is flimsy and ephemeral. Rather, fashion has the best chance of making it into the archive, which seeks to preserve cultural markers of any given time. Fashion allows for values to be unequal, the basis of the new, its encouragement of elitism actually permitting value-making to run smoothly. Fashion is anti-utopian and anti-totalitarian, never claiming to be permanently significant. Fashion arises neither by accident, passivity, calculation, nor greed. Its motivation is frustration with cultural banality. And it offers a window into just how difficult it is to attain originality, the product of "very special efforts" not easily seen by those who do not work as professionals in the culture industry.[81]

The path to the new is through the boundary that lies between the archive and the profane. The Western archive is a vast storehouse with a quota. Like Noah's ark, it only has room for one of each kind and will reject anything redundant or superfluous. Whatever is not in this archive is profane—without value, description, interest, or relevance, relegated to a space outside culture. Yet, the profane realm holds resource deposits. And there is a permeable boundary between the profane and the archive. For Groys, there is nothing beyond this interdependence. To see the profane realm as somehow more authentic is to ignore that profanity is made so *because* of the archive. Truly new art does not become valuable because of its resemblance to art but because of its resemblance to something just outside of it.

Things do not pass across this boundary equally. Some differences are relevant and valuable, some aren't. Innovation in culture is rare but must happen at some point. And when things pass across the boundary, they do not pass only one way. Existing values are devalued when something profane attains value. The pressure of certain aspects of the profane on high culture does not make the boundary crossing happen. And the boundary may be crossed for any number of reasons—compassion for the profane, careerism, idealism—but this doesn't mean the crossing is successful. A potentially new thing carries tension, but usually, according to Groys, it is easier to see how something is profane, rather than how its profanity may be set against existing cultural memory to form the valuable new. Eventually, the tension of the valuable new diminishes. "Eventually," Groys writes, "the next innovation comes due."[82]

Any gesture in which "worldly things" are equated with any kind of sacred tradition is, for Groys, the characteristic, driving force behind all European culture.[83] Notably, culture never fully lets in the actual profane, but rather representations and theories of it that bring the profane closer to the valued archive—but not inside of it. A new gesture does not reveal something absent from culture. Rather, it allows culture to refresh itself, by allowing it to be observed, via the gesture, from a vantage point outside itself.

Does the economy of the new persist in contemporary culture, where nothing seems new anymore? Has the inrush of globalization and digital culture, with their presumed multiplicity of perspectives, eliminated the profane and, with it, cultural innovation? Has this elimination been aided by liberal democracy, which appears to lift all taboos and censorship? Has culture otherwise moved to the profane so aggressively, stylizing everything as profane, that what constitutes a cultural object cannot be separated from the profane?

None of this has quite happened, argues Groys. First, profane things are never taken into culture in their original form. European artists merely took elements of the African masks they appropriated, not the essence; even entire masks taken by institutions have been stripped of their ceremonial function. Western culture only takes the thing it can contrast with itself, leaving the profane to still exist, untouched. There is no state in Western culture in which everything can be new, leaving, by logical extension, nothing to be new. Value is always bestowed with a kind of exclusivity, and the profane thing does not share space with everything already in the archive but vies for power and influence to ensure tactical superiority in its struggle to enter the archive. No valorization can grant a work totalizing power. And to view the profane as the site of a deeper truth is, for Groys, just "the promise of another sort of power, strength, universality, and exclusivity"[84]—another realm of valuation that aims to replace, and be, the archive.

In the climax of *On the New*, Groys considers the culture industry's obsession with anything that appears to be its other as a kind of death drive. Of modernist avant-garde movements like Futurism, which called for the destruction of museums, Groys writes:

> We might say that the nihilistic and universalist ideological movements of modernity act, their sometimes extremely violent assaults on culture notwithstanding, as conjuring rituals that symbolically effect its total destruction so as to check that destruction and, ultimately, ward it off.[85]

So it is that when profane things are brought into culture as new, they are called in, only for certain of their attributes to be cast out. Western culture is a ritual, equating the profane with the valued not to topple hierarchy, but to stabilize it, away from nature.

The profane will never be depleted. An accelerated contemporary economy of the new simply accelerates the production of the profane. Cultural trash, literal landfills and wastelands, come to represent the realm outside the culturally valuable in a way that is, for Groys, more profane than "Amazonia's virgin nature."[86] Waste is to contemporary culture what nature was to the Renaissance: it represents the power of culture to make anything sacred. Waste as the new profane realm for European culture also allows for further repudiation of the Christian church under liberalism. Nothing is resurrected from a junkyard—it just comes back around. There remains an unchangeable destiny within culture, however, that is fiercely Christian. Because every innovation comes at a cost—any profane thing that enters the archive must take the place of something already there, which in turn must be devalued—every innovation constitutes both a sacrifice and a conquest. If, under secular liberalism, the cultural archive is the only means by which to attain the eternal life once promised by God and heaven, it must have a corresponding Satan and hell to make it real. In Groys's words, Western culture has "no choice but to love its enemies."[87]

3
The Whole Earth

America has no memory.

—US actor-playwright Wallace Shawn, to former
Vanity Fair editor Tina Brown, January 31, 1984[1]

Once, European culture was valued and US culture profane. Then, European culture was profane and US culture valued.

Andreas Reckwitz's book *The Invention of Creativity* explains how the new, through our current fixation with creativity, operates to precise social utility and effect. Creativity is now normalized. US socioeconomic theorist Richard Florida's bestselling 2002 book *The Rise of the Creative Class*, for instance, extols artists as socio-economic innovators.[2] Yet, the post-Enlightenment concept of creativity emerges from the frenetic, compulsive understanding of the European and British Romantics, who believed inspiration could be encountered, but never held. Indeed, many Romantics warned that creativity could quickly become anti-social and destructive—drug-like, first fêting the ego, then annihilating it. The US–European culture wars of the 20th century were a turning point, when creativity became the subject of capture. For Reckwitz, art and function began to merge into a *"creativity dispositif,"* where creativity is the primary means by which to determine value.[3] The focus of this *dispositif* is art's ability to generate ideas, empower its makers, and have an impact on an audience's emotional responses, through stimulation, mood alteration, and the provocation of reactions like enthusiasm, calm, and shock—all micro versions of the annihilation of which the Romantics spoke.[4] In Reckwitz's *dispositif*, creativity fortifies. No longer a narcotic, it is a pharmaceutical, a vitamin.

The US artist Jackson Pollock is a pivotal figure in Reckwitz's book, and at the center of French scholar Serge Guilbaut's neglected 1983 study *How New York Stole the Idea of Modern Art: Abstract Expressionism, Freedom, and the Cold War*. Guilbaut dissects the oft-told story of a group of male, mid-20th-century US painters, several of them from working-class and/or immigrant families—Jackson Pollock, Mark Rothko, Willem de Kooning—who changed the avant-garde forever with a renegade, non-representative style that included paint drips all over the canvas, brush strokes evoking muralism and street art, and blocks of pure colour. These painters, the story goes, changed not just the direction of the avant-garde, but also its central location, bringing artistic experimentation to the USA from Europe, and establishing New York as the West's new avant-garde capital, snatching the crown from Paris. For Guilbaut, the story, now a myth, is instructive in ways that are underdiscussed. Because myths are received as kinds of facts, their origins and purposes are often neglected.[5]

It should seem strange that US art went abstract in the 1940s. Established US fine art had always been figurative: drawn from reality, following folk traditions, and influenced by cultural and political socialism. Through the Federal Art Project (FAP), the Works Progress Administration employed millions under Democratic president Franklin Delano Roosevelt's 1930s New Deal, including Pollock, Rothko, and other soon-to-be Abstract Expressionists. One of Pollock's paintings for the FAP, *The Cotton Pickers* (c.1935), recalls Courbet and Jean-François Millet, French painters who made figurative depictions of the working class into avant-garde gestures in another country and century. Pollock's early painting also shows the influence of US regionalist painter Thomas Hart Benton, who mentored Pollock and whose depictions of the "American scene" drove the currents of a developing, if not intellectually respected, idea of US culture,[6] which included jazz and Hollywood film. At the same time as the soon-to-be Abstract Expressionists were completing figurative work for the FAP, Cubists, Surrealists, and Dadaists continued to solidify Paris as an avant-garde hotbed. Plain were the distinctions between the two. France maintained an ineffable, elite type of newness that the USA, still a frontier backwater, could not yet grasp.

Talk of "crisis" and "late capitalism" is not unique to our time. As Guilbaut notes, such talk was a hallmark of the 1930s, with its Depression and attendant rise of fascist governments. These two massive events met with an increasingly global response, fascism seeing a significant, cross-factional resistance through a Soviet strategy of class collaboration, which proposed an alliance with liberal intellectuals, making both factions revolutionaries in the fight against fascism, in a movement that became known as the Popular Front. The Front demanded unity at all costs, prompting Western intellectuals with communist affiliations to consider culture in nationalist terms, and thus as an anti-fascist strategy.[7]

By the mid- to late 1930s, this alliance was already under strain. Joseph Stalin's Moscow Trials brutally attempted to silence the resistance of Leon Trotsky and his followers. In 1939, Soviet Russia and Nazi Germany signed the Molotov–Ribbentrop Pact of non-aggression.[8] The curdling of Soviet communism led to a breakdown of Front unity in the USA and to a systematic intellectual querying: can art contribute to political change and national identity and still be progressive—experimental, avant-garde? Are the middle or working classes the best audiences for the most important types of art? Can, and should, art be affiliated with any politics, or should it remain independent at all costs? When is artistic independence a sham?

Given, among other things, the propagandistic use of art in service of totalitarianism, art-extolling US intellectuals began, in Guilbaut's story, to question their communist affiliations and the regionalist, working-class representations that came with them. Freedom—to express and create, embedded in Reckwitz's *creativity dispositif*—gained importance, over representation. Freedom was also a virtue of the fringe European art movements Dada and Surrealism, but would take a much different form in the US avant-garde.

Still, in publications like *The Partisan Review* (*TPR*), highbrow US culture of open communist affiliation turned across the Atlantic for guidance.[9] Trotsky himself contributed to *TPR*, where he stressed the need for art to maintain independence, precisely so that it may be revolutionary and in dialogue with freedom. In his commissioned 1938 letter to *TPR* titled "Art and Politics," Trotsky compared art to science, claiming that both "cannot tolerate" taking orders from anyone, and that "creation" should not be conformist but faithful only to itself.[10] In "Towards a Free Revolutionary Art," a 1938 manifesto published in *TPR* signed by Mexican muralist Diego Rivera and French Surrealist André Breton and prepared in collaboration with Trotsky, there is similar wording: "True art is unable *not* to be revolutionary, *not* to aspire to a complete and radical reconstruction of society."[11] A "true" aspiration to create replaces a more corruptible aspiration to make political change. The creative pursuit of truth, whatever that means, inspires freedom, and is authentically new.

In 1939, *TPR* published the essay "Avant-Garde and Kitsch" by the US critic Clement Greenberg. Decades later, the essay entered art-history curricula as a pamphlet for the ideology of Abstract Expressionism. One of the most influential art critics of the 20th century, with all the associated preferences and scorn this entails, Greenberg does not thrill the contemporary imagination. Yet "Avant-Garde and Kitsch" remains relevant. Guilbaut calls Greenberg more pessimistic than Trotsky, Breton, and Rivera, but Greenberg's essay is still a manifesto, *The Rise of the Creative Class* of its day. For Guilbaut, it marks nothing less than the "de-Marxization" of the avant-garde in US culture.[12]

Greenberg's essay attempts to pin down the limits of the freedom Trotsky et al. urged. The avant-garde, Greenberg writes, comes out of crisis—"the decay of our present society"—and as such is responsive and not entirely free, at least not materially.[13] Greenberg identifies the ruling class's decline, which is important, because this class was a driver of Western culture, even of revolution. Radicals may repudiate this class, but it held the purse strings of the avant-garde: in Greenberg's famous words, "an umbilical cord of gold."[14] The crisis of culture in 1939 was, for Greenberg, nothing less than a culture war. The ruling class had abandoned the avant-garde and left culture to the masses, who, for Greenberg, were indifferent to the growth and development of new ideas. Without ruling-class funding, however, culture falls to bad taste or kitsch—mass produced versions of high culture, such as porcelain figurines of Renaissance sculptures. (Greenberg's definition is expansive and includes, hilariously, the *New Yorker* magazine.[15])

Greenberg's culture war is between different types of newness. Newness itself is not at issue; it will always be the primary value in any capitalist society. Rather, the war is between the new in its authentic (avant-garde) and fake (kitsch) forms. For pessimistic Greenberg, choosing the avant-garde will not create utopia, but will make the best of a bad situation. At least the avant-garde keeps things going. The most important function of the avant-garde is not to experiment but to keep culture alive and active through crisis. Kitsch, the most lucrative aspect of the culture industry, keeps things going as well—perversely, in Greenberg's view, looting the new for its "twists," which are "watered down and served up" to a general audience.[16]

Like the Judeo-Christian God, Greenberg's avant-garde artist attempts to make things by virtue of their own independent existence. This often ends up as abstraction: works that are not *about* things other than what they inherently *are*. For Greenberg, such works are unironically "pure," but not totalitarian, because they are "innocent"—as opposed to kitsch, which is made by cynical manufacturers.[17] Greenberg's avant-garde is a system, put deliberately in place to save culture with the necessary help of the ruling class. Kitsch is also a system, also put in place by capital, but it imposes the new to stunt, not to create. Kitsch is "the first universal culture ever beheld"[18]—and that, for Greenberg, is not a good thing.

Yet, the avant-garde has its own inspiring universalism: persistent creativity. Greenberg is not Trotsky. Greenberg's avant-garde artist, at the brink of World War II, could not, Guilbaut writes, engage in politics and culture at once, but was trying to save the furniture in a burning house.[19] Greenberg demonstrates the impetus for the avant-garde to abandon radical politics: the de-Marxization of the avant-garde, an old recipe "served up with a new sauce."[20] In his essay "The Late Thirties in New York," Greenberg writes, "Some day it will have to be told how anti-Stalinism which started out more or less as Trotskyism turned into art for art's sake and thereby cleared the way, heroically, for what was to come."[21]

Well into the 1930s, the US avant-garde still struggled to gain international respect. Guilbaut relates a pronounced negative reaction to the 1938 "American Art" painting show in Paris, which, according to the French critic François Fosca, was not new, simply reminding critics of what they weren't seeing, and liked better: fun, zippy American movies.[22] For the French, painting expressed taste and enduring refinement, impossible for the USA, given its youth. Movies, architecture, jazz were the only US cultural forms worthwhile, because they were *actually* new: exuberant, unselfconscious, uncouth. Back in 1917, Duchamp had already called US industry its best avant-garde product, claiming "the only works of art America has given are her plumbing and her bridges."[23] In celebrating the USA's mass culture and deriding its painting, France inadvertently set the stage for the USA's takeover, a bragging hare in the value archive, ignorant of the persistent, profane tortoise approaching.

World War II destroyed France's economy and threatened many of its cultural traditions. After this disaster, US painters could finally eschew regionalism and be international: general qualities beginning to define the USA at this time. The new that would drive the emerging US avant-garde would depend both on the profanity of its beginnings—subjugation of Black and Indigenous cultures—and of its future ambitions, to be a cultural proxy for the entire world, a no-place and everyplace at once, not international but universal. The new US avant-garde would be an individual dream, but also fundamentally homogenous, a self-sustaining system that altered the world without having to change the USA's founding complexion at all. It happened in lockstep with the country's self-positioning as top global superpower for the rest of the 20th century, and would eventually become a kind of liberal kitsch.

* * *

The new US avant-garde heeded Greenberg in its special attention to class. Specifically, it sought a museum of its own. In a 1933 report to trustees, the Museum of Modern Art (MoMA)'s founding director Alfred H. Barr Jr. transparently identified its audience as a specific hierarchy in which trustees are first, followed by scholars, dealers, philanthropists, businesspeople, students, and, last, the general public.²⁴ At the 1939 opening of the MoMA's West 53rd Street location in New York, where it remains today, trustee Paul J. Sachs remarked: "The Museum of Modern Art has a duty to the great public. But in serving an elite it will reach, better than in any other way, the great general public by means of work done to meet the most exacting standards of an elite."²⁵

The 1930s MoMA, bankrolled by the Rockefellers, largely exhibited and touted the European avant-garde. But it would soon be the site of a paradigm shift. Throughout that decade, Barr called the MoMA an "experimental laboratory."²⁶ In 1942, collector, patron, and curator Peggy Guggenheim, whose Art of This Century gallery was MoMA's spiritual partner just a few blocks up the street, called her space "a research lab for new ideas."²⁷

By the time the USA joined the war in 1941, obliteration was the order of the day. Paris, the capital of modern Western culture, had fallen to the Nazis. The US press characterized fascism as against all culture, ignoring fascism's fetish for neoclassicism. Of course, the US press was really defending and upholding modernism as anti-fascist culture: before the war, the Nazis had notoriously disparaged modernism as degenerate. As Guilbaut notes, urgent ideological essays in the *Partisan Review* were one thing, the transformative impact of a world war quite another.²⁸ The stage for the USA's ascendance as the new site of the modernist avant-garde had been set.

In her 1998 book *The Power of Display: A History of Exhibition Installations at the Museum of Modern Art*, US scholar Mary Anne Staniszewski puts exhibition design at the early MoMA alongside other modern phenomena, including department stores and mass media.²⁹ *The Power of Display* begins with a quote from one of Barr's idols, Herbert Bayer, printing and advertising director of Germany's Bauhaus art and design school, the hub of the applied-arts wing of the European avant-garde that did much to define the look and style of the 20th century. Bayer writes:

> Exhibition design has evolved as a new discipline, as an apex of all media and powers of communication and of collective efforts and effects. The total application of all plastic and psychological means (more than anything else) makes exhibition design an intensified and new language.[30]

Here is Reckwitz's *creativity dispositif* in its infancy.

European avant-garde exhibition design made things new by putting them in relation. Austrian designer Friedrich Kiesler and Russian designer El Lissitzky saw their shows as "integrated interiors,"[31] the parts of which could be combined and interact with viewers to create new encounters—a material version of Wittgenstein's theory of language, or an extension of composer Richard Wagner's purpose-built theatre at Bayreuth, Germany, and his idea of a *gesamtkunstwerk*, an artwork with multisensory, multidisciplinary impact. Staniszewski uses evocative diction for European avant-garde exhibition design, which incorporated raised walkways and movable structures for art objects: "an organic unfolding of aesthetic spirit"; "a fertile ground for... creativity"; an "infinite" space suggesting the contemporary and the prehistoric at once.[32] The viewer is totally immersed, anonymous. But they are also acutely aware of their individual power to consume, shape, and choose.

An environment thus conceived also suggests the colonial-legal concepts *terra incognita* and *terra nullius*, of unknown and empty lands respectively, from which the new is meant to come, in a *creatio ex nihilo*. The MoMA's mythology includes the trips Barr took with Philip Johnson, part of MoMA's architecture department, across the Atlantic to visit the

Bauhaus and other temples of the European avant-garde—effective voyages of discovery. Such trips may recall Mark Twain's concept of US travellers in Europe as "innocents abroad."[33] However, Barr and Johnson were no innocents, coming instead to study, repossess, and remake old-world culture—a colonialism protectively turned inside out. Indeed, although such trips contextualize Guilbaut's story of how New York stole the idea of modern art, they have persisted, with contemporary curators travelling to "biennial shop" the world for new shows and artists. Barr and Johnson also brought the European avant-garde to the USA through the importation of its living architects and designers for exhibitions and projects, from Walter Gropius, head of the Bauhaus, to architect Mies van der Rohe. World War II simply aided this project, with avant-garde artist-émigrés flocking to the USA, and to New York in particular.

Herbert Bayer became a US citizen during World War II but his influence on MoMA, where he would himself design exhibitions, began in the 1930s. In Bayer's exhibition-design drawings, a cartoon figure, meant to represent an everyviewer, is placed on a platform and given "360 degrees field of vision" of the gallery, able to see panels on the ceiling, floors, and walls.[34] The figure says unsurprising things about the modern understanding of the gallery-goer: formally attired in a suit, male, upper-middle class, of average-ideal height. The figure's defining characteristic is that his head is simply an eyeball.

The MoMA visitor is empowered to see everything at once, yet carefully guided through both new and old, as if by an anthropologist. (Bayer employed footprints in his exhibition designs, also a motif of the early MoMA.) Bayer's viewer suggests the sensibility of Greenberg's avant-garde artist: detached from the outside world with access to certain truths, but also unable to change the forces guiding him, exploring reality by questioning seeing, without being seen. Staniszewski notes that most exhibition photography from the MoMA contains no humans, with the occasional exception of women, children, Indigenous communities, and dignitaries, exceptions within the gaze of Bayer's viewer and thus separated from his identity.[35]

Barr, Johnson, and others at the MoMA ultimately refined the exhibition designs of the European avant-garde for their own purposes, but Bayer's everyviewer remained influential. The *gesamtkunstwerk* of the MoMA was subtle—neutral, minimal, eye-level installation—and appealed to a standardized viewer, meant to be aesthetically, if not necessarily politically, neutral. For Staniszewski, the MoMA came to embody national concerns, treating the viewer as if they had "an ahistorical, unified sovereignty of the self—much like the art objects the spectator was viewing," with the works in turn anthropomorphized to greet the viewer, putting the viewer and the art "face to face" and "eye to eye" in a kind of curatorial diplomacy.[36]

The chaos and tumult of US capitalism, its lack of refinement, was, it turned out, a boon for aesthetics. Such were the ideas espoused by the likes of Samuel Kootz, a businessman-cum-art-dealer who wrote a letter published in the *New York Times* in 1941, characterizing Paris as the antagonist of new young America and who, after the publication of this letter, was invited to curate a show at Macy's department store.[37] The art market further democratized, and although the middle class, who still liked regionalism and realism, were not buying the same art as the upper class, who liked abstraction, or at least were told to, the tension between the markets created healthy competition and class one-upmanship. The busy day-to-day of many Americans meant that art buyers wanted to be fed knowledge to save time. The middle class looked to *LIFE* magazine, the upper class to MoMA.

In Guilbaut's story, moments like Kootz's letter add up. The Abstract Expressionists themselves did the work of repudiating politics entirely, while their work became increasingly political. In the 1943 catalog for an exhibition by the Federation of American Painters and Sculptors's *American Modern Artists*, the painter Barnett Newman railed against the patriotic *Artists for Victory* show at the Metropolitan Museum of Art.[38] Newman, with fellow painters Adolph Gottlieb and Rothko, also railed against a bad review in the *New York Times*, writing that Abstract Expressionism was "an adventure into an unknown world," a dream quest aligned more with "primitives and archaic art" than with any "American scene."[39] At the same time, Republican politician and lawyer Wendell Willkie's best-selling 1943 book *One World* argued the USA had a responsibility to create a harmonious, technologically connected global society after defeating the Nazis.[40] (In 1947, a French lawyer wrote an anonymous letter to the magazine *The Nation* suggesting One World was becoming One American World.[41])

After World War II, the Marshall Plan followed, an expansive US strategy to give aid to Europe that affirmed the USA's ambitions as a postwar superpower. As a prelude to the Plan, the 1946 Blum–Byrnes Accord, signed to help a war-torn France, contained a buried clause that prohibited the French from showing more than four films of their own per financial quarter.[42] In 1947, Pollock, de Kooning, and Rothko all worked on paintings where no form was recognizable; shortly thereafter, Kootz curated a show at the Maeght Gallery in Paris, with indirect government backing. French critics responded to Kootz's show with defensive *ennui*, claiming all avant-gardes were over.[43] In a way, they were. In 1949, historian Arthur Schlesinger Jr. published his book *The Vital Center: The Politics of Freedom*, a hardened postwar argument, 30 years before Thatcher, that positioned liberal capitalism as the only alternative in a world of totalitarianism, chaos, uncertainty, and anxiety—the last avant-garde.

In this way, US culture came to trust the perpetual revaluation of its own profanity, to which it laid zealous claim. Pollock's painting, *She-Wolf*, was made in 1943, exhibited by Guggenheim that same year, and sold to MoMA the year after, the paint still fresh, with Guggenheim co-facilitating the sale. Soon after, *She-Wolf* appeared in the pages of *Harper's Bazaar*, with a quote from Pollock saying he "had to paint it" and that any attempt to say something about it "could only destroy it."[44] Greenberg wrote warnings in *The Nation*, cautioning that any company that took up the avant-garde style failed to realize that "to be for something uncritically does more harm in the end than being against it."[45] Greenberg further cautioned:

> It is in the very nature of academicism to be pessimistic, for it believes history to be a repetitious and monotonous decline from a former golden age. The avant-garde on the other hand believes that history is creative, always evolving novelty out of itself. And where there is novelty there is hope.[46]

Greenberg had perhaps underestimated himself. In 1964, Danto defined the concept of an "artworld," carried from Europe to the USA, and responding specifically to the Pop artist Andy Warhol but also to another Pop artist, Robert Rauschenberg, whose *Bed* (1955) used a quilt and sheet as a canvas. By the 1990s, Danto came to understand his art world as eschatological: theory would soon be all there was left from its experiments. Yet, even in 1964, Danto defined this place as "something the eye cannot descry—an atmosphere of artistic theory, a knowledge of history of art."[47] The art world was a system, a way of understanding contemporary culture entirely. It was not, could not be, merely visual.

Abstract Expressionism was part of Danto's accretive vision of the art world, but it also rewrote the past, shoring European art history against present works, with an expansive "now" of artistic creation imagining any future it might inhabit. As long as the system remained independent, it could keep producing new things. The concept domesticated by Barr and Johnson at the MoMA, and popping up in cities across the USA, fortified art, protecting it from ever getting old, or from ever directly reaching the masses, who at the time were increasingly suburban. Such fortification nonetheless welcomed, even encouraged, those beyond its walls to recognize, acknowledge, and use it for what it was.

An independent US avant-garde, slightly next door to the masses, remained new by keeping the class divide in place. In 1949, *LIFE* ran a feature on Pollock that mocked him, just as it would run a 1959 feature on the Beat Generation that mocked them. Guilbaut notes that the publicity *LIFE* gave Pollock allowed his dealer Betty Parsons to sell almost all his works she exhibited that year.[48] The previous year, *LIFE* hosted a panel on "The Strange Art of Today" and recorded the response of one Mr. Duthui to Pollock's *Cathedral*: "I find it quite lovely. It is new to me."[49] But it didn't have to be lovely to be new. Nor did it have to feel significant. The masses might take Abstract Expressionism or leave it, but they were told to respect it, as they did many faddish commodities. They knew what it stood for.

* * *

In 1942, Pollock hosted the German émigré painter Hans Hofmann in his studio, the two introduced by Pollock's partner, the painter Lee Krasner. Noting the lack of realist depictions in Pollock's work, Hofmann reputedly asked, "Do you work from nature?" Pollock reputedly answered, "I am nature."⁵⁰

In 1946, the artist Ad Reinhardt published a cartoon in *Newsweek* called "The Rescue of Art" and captioned "Timeless Political Cartoon." The cartoon depicted a Lillian Gish-type girl standing like a motionless doll on a track with a train approaching from behind. The girl is labelled "ART," and the train has eight, trailing labels attached to it: "BANALITY," "PREJUDICE," "LINGUISTIC STEREO-TYPES," "DRINK," "INFERIORITY COMPLEXES," "CORRUPTION," "MONEY-GRUBBING," and "SIN." A well-dressed boy labelled "ABSTRACT ART" dodges out of the bushes to save her.⁵¹

Guilbaut uses Reinhardt's cartoon to demonstrate how, after World War II, New York seemed to be completely overtaken by abstract art, which was associated with any number of virtues. (The cartoon has recently appeared online, an ahead-of-its-time meme appearing to critique wokeness, the contemporary, online version of 1990s political correctness.) Since the boy comes from the bush, the cartoon also demonstrates how abstraction joins a line of profane heroes, pushed from nature to help keep art alive.

W. Jackson Rushing's 1995 study *Native American Art and the New York Avant-Garde: A History of Cultural Primitivism* does not begin in 1930s New York but in the 1910s, with the artist colonies and aristocrat frontierspeople that settled among the Pueblo Nations around Santa Fe and Taos, New Mexico. Here, many who would later influence the New York avant-garde were seeing in Indigenous forms and designs natural unity, mythic and psychic power, and the very origins of human consciousness.⁵²

Often shuttling to and from New York, these settlers had a progressive, bohemian vision. In attacking bourgeois values, they also actively contributed to a national project in their attempt to locate an authentic, marketable avant-garde.[53] The settlers turned their gazes not just to Tewa, Zuni, and other Pueblo Nations, but to nations great distances away: Kwakwaka'wakw (Kwakiutl), Tlingit, Haida, and Inuit. They bundled all into what Rushing sees as a cabinet of curiosities, a curated collection speaking to the settlers' own imperatives. Constructing the scaffolding for Abstract Expressionism, these settlers transposed the European avant-garde's use of African and Asian cultures, and the "noble savage" of German romanticist author Karl May. Rushing's is the little-told story of how the US West remains site and lifeblood of its culture industry, with northern New Mexico the missing chapter among Hollywood, New York, and Silicon Valley.

The Taos and Santa Fe colonies' gaze on Pueblo Nations is a welter of Western ideas of the new. There was indeed a new art emerging among Pueblo Nations around the settler colonies at the time, the result of past and present contact. San Ildefonso Pueblo labourers such as Alfredo (Wen Tsireh) Montoya were, beginning in 1909, employed at Rito de Los Frijoles excavation site, where an ancient community house was being unearthed. During their work, the labourers encountered pre-contact murals, which later inspired them to make watercolours, the medium having been introduced by settler educators in the day schools—notably at the Santa Fe Indian School by superintendent John DeHuff and his wife, teacher Elizabeth Willis DeHuff, who encouraged students to make art about their heritage, despite strict US government acculturation policies.[54] (The DeHuffs were later dismissed from their jobs for these efforts.) A community of Pueblo painters formed, including Awa Tsireh (Cattail Bird) and Tonita Peña (Quah Ah) of San Ildefonso Pueblo; Velino Shije Herrera of Zia Pueblo; and Fred Kabotie (Naqavoy'ma), Hopi, whom the government had sent to Santa Fe Indian School to acculturate, and who went on to become an internationally renowned artist.

Alice Corbin Henderson, a Chicagoan who had moved to Santa Fe with her husband, wrote an article on Awa Tsireh for the *New York Times* in 1925, remarking on his works:

> I thought... that they pointed a new direction; and indeed, Alfonso's [i.e., Awa Tsireh's] example proved to be the start for a genuine new development of Pueblo art. Other Pueblo artists... began to record their more realistic impressions of the life about them, and soon there was veritably a "new school" of aboriginal water-color artists.[55]

It's a story at least as old as the colonial Americas. The new art of the Pueblo school was an opportunity for settlers in retreat from the hustle and bustle of the urban to contemplate a more authentic way of being. Seventy years prior, the transcendentalists—the original US avant-garde—had gathered at Brook Farm in Massachusetts, their vision influenced by the utopian socialism of French philosopher Charles Fourier.

In New Mexico, Edgar L. Hewett, an instrumental patron of the Santa Fe and Taos colonies, promoted tourism of the area by bolstering its artistic reputation. In a 1918 article, Hewett wrote that "ultra-modernists were groping to return to the primitive conventionalism and symbolism of the Pueblo."[56] Mary Hunter Austin, women's rights advocate and co-founder of the original art colony in Carmel, California, compared the work and culture of northern New Mexico Indigenous peoples to Ancient Greek and Egyptian civilizations, envisioning a museum of Indigenous art that would support local communities while building an aesthetic identity for the USA.[57] Mabel Dodge Luhan, who founded the Taos colony, and whose house, where the British novelist D.H. Lawrence and others visited, stands today as a tourist attraction, wrote that the "Southwest may be the land of the new birth, of the synthetic American culture we have all desired."[58] In 1926, New Yorker John Sloan, founding member of the Whitney Studio Club, who would play a pivotal role in bringing a pan-Indigenous vision to the New York art world, proclaimed the death of modern art but the survival of "ultramodern art," positing that if there was ever to be an authentic US art, it would come from Indigenous New Mexico.[59] In 1922, Holger Cahill, later director of the FAP, wrote that although Western culture had built a "sordid Industrial Babel," Pueblo culture had, in contrast, an "aestheticism and deeply religious feeling."[60] Painter Marsden Hartley called the Indigenous artist, broadly, "the one truly indigenous religionist and esthete of America."[61]

The settlers' project often took the form of well-meaning cultural advocacy and, later, of full-blown existential healing and liberation.[62] Many of the ceremonial objects that became lodestars for the early to mid-20th-century New York avant-garde had, of course, their origin in colonial theft. As historian Tina Loo points out, the 450 items from Dan Cranmer's 1921 potlatch among the Alert Bay Kwakwaka'wakw—a nation of great interest to Barnett Newman, who curated shows of Northwest Coast art—were confiscated by law and taken to what is now the Canadian Museum of History in Ottawa and the Royal Ontario Museum in Toronto. They began to be returned from the 1960s onward only after advocacy from the nation, whose members appeared in Ottawa to demand the objects back.[63]

In November 1931, the "Exposition of Indian Tribal Arts" at New York's Grand Central Art Galleries intended to show Indigenous objects "as art—not ethnology."[64] According to Sloan and anthropologist and novelist Oliver La Farge, the show's organizers, the works on display were "an expression of a continuing vigor seeking new outlets and not, like ours, a search for a release from exhaustion."[65] The new, found in culture, would renew. Brooklyn Museum curator Herbert J. Spinden wrote that the sacred night chant of the Navajo would become part of "our national literature as mysterious and beautiful dramas which somehow prefigure the American ideal," and that Indigenous cultures would "enrich the oversoul of society"[66]—a reference to the transcendental ideas of the poet Ralph Waldo Emerson, who did not join, and in fact criticized, Brook Farm.

The enlisting of Indigenous cultural objects for the well-being of US nationalism was solidified by MoMA curator René d'Harnoncourt's important 1941 exhibition *Indian Art of the United States*. D'Harnoncourt had been the general manager of the Indian Arts and Crafts Board, an initiative of Roosevelt's new commissioner for the Bureau of Indian Affairs John Collier to further integrate Indigenous culture into that of colonial America. According to Rushing, Collier had faith in Swiss psychiatrist and psychoanalyst Carl Jung's theories of consciousness transformation via so-called ancient values, and saw in Indigenous nations a spiritual ballast for the modern world,[67] part of a larger intellectual fetishization of the Americas, which included Mexican mural painting, another influence on Abstract Expressionism. (In 1939, F.A. Whiting Jr. wrote an editorial in *Magazine of Art* about the art of the Americas titled "The New World Is Still New."[68])

"Indian Art of the United States," its title changed from the original "Indian Art in North America," gathered nations and spanned time periods.[69] Rushing sees three categories in d'Harnoncourt's show: pre-contact objects that d'Harnoncourt would show "only as art for art's sake," decontextualized; current objects from living nations that would, to the best of MoMA's ability, be shown contextualized, as these nations used them; and contemporary art by Indigenous artists, including a piece by Awa Tsireh, on loan from Abby Aldrich Rockefeller's collection, in the recontextualized setting of the modern

MoMA—"very contemporary and Fifth Avenue in the best sense of the word" according to d'Harnoncourt.[70]

Here was the merging of *l'art pour l'art* with functionality in a way perhaps only the MoMA could do. Avant-garde praxis put "real-life" objects in an art context, not just to startle bourgeois audiences but to reawaken them to new values. D'Harnoncourt's displays included the use of Indigenous objects and materials in industrial fashion design and home décor, for instance.[71] Again, like Duchamp, La Farge found that the works in the show, "some material, some intangible… can stand comparison with skyscrapers or the present apex of white civilization in Europe."[72]

In response to d'Harnoncourt's exhibition, artist Max Weber wrote to Alfred H. Barr that "we have the *real* Surrealists right here in America."[73] Accordingly, as the 1940s progressed, and despite d'Harnoncourt's attempts at museum-situated cultural contextualization in the exhibition, the Abstract Expressionists moved Indigenous art further from its creators and into the fortified US individualism that excluded them. The "primordial," the "primitive," and "atavistic myth" became obsessions of Abstract Expressionist painters. Gestures toward Indigenous art as both very US American and very universal, transcending history, became more commonplace.[74] In *System and Dialectics of Art*, a 1937 book popular among the New York avant-garde, John D. Graham wrote that "creation is the production of new authentic values by delving into memories of immemorial past and expressing them in terms of pure form (in space and matter) in order to project them into the clarities of the future."[75]

Focus on the self and its journeys quickly displaced any attention to Indigenous ways of knowing. As Rushing notes, Newman was fascinated with Northwest Coast totems and pre-contact cultures, seeing in both the "transcending [of] time and place."[76] Alongside the Jungian cast of the Abstract

Expressionists' valuations were Nietzsche's Apollonian and Dionysian, the former's imperative of light, insight, and self-improvement—the sacred—and the latter's terror, chaos, and self-annihilation—the profane. Artists such as Gottlieb and Pollock would continue to allude to Indigenous art in their work. Gottlieb included motifs like petroglyphs, claiming they were the "global language of art."[77] Pollock admired the technique of Navajo sand painting, which may have influenced his drip paintings, and of which he likely saw a live performance at d'Harnoncourt's exhibition.[78]

* * *

Pop replaced Abstract Expressionism and was not that different from Dada, although its subjects were the products of US, not European, industry: film stars, billboards, magazines, and TV advertisements. Pop was the culture industry looking inward at itself and declaring that it had become American culture, full stop, swallowing the avant-garde whole.

US critic Calvin Tomkins's 1962 book *The Bride and the Bachelors: Five Masters of the Avant-Garde* takes place in the avant-garde that New York had built. Duchamp is Tomkins's bride—his title is from a Duchamp work—because Duchamp had put New York on the map as an avant-garde capital even before World War I. Duchamp's *Nude Descending a Staircase No. 2* was a *succès de scandale* at the 1913 Armory Show;[79] the sale of this and associated works allowed Duchamp to emigrate to the city for the first time in 1915.[80] Duchamp returned to New York during World War II,[81] to stay through the 1960s, his studio famously sited on 14th Street in Greenwich Village.[82] Duchamp's reputation, Tomkins writes, had always been greater in New York than in Paris. In his own avant-garde way, Duchamp was an emblem of liberal democracy in America:

Even the Abstract Expressionists, whose intensely "retinal" painting is about as far as possible from the Duchamp concept of art as a mental act, seem to go along with Willem de Kooning's celebrated remark that "Duchamp is a one-man movement, but a movement for each person and open to everybody."[83]

Robert Rauschenberg, the last of Tomkins's bachelors, combined Abstract Expressionism and Duchamp's particular idea of Dada to make Pop. Tomkins portrays an opening at Rauschenberg's 1963 retrospective at New York's Jewish Museum, where *Bed* appeared, and in which the artist determined to sell his art as product. In Tomkins's vignette, the museum's patrons are for the most part bewildered, bored, and shocked. A woman approaches Rauschenberg and asks why he only likes ugly things. ("She really wanted to know," Rauschenberg tells Tomkins.[84]) In response, Rauschenberg asks the patron why, exactly, she finds his materials so ugly. She tells him that they are random and have no meaning. Rauschenberg says to Tomkins:

> So I told her that if I were to describe the way she was dressed, it might sound very much like what she'd been saying. For instance, she had feathers on her head. And she had this enamel brooch with a picture of *The Blue Boy* on it pinned to her breast. And around her neck she had on what she would call mink but what could also be described as the skin of a dead animal.[85]

The woman comes around. Rauschenberg praises her intelligence: "She hadn't been able to *look* at the pictures until somebody helped her."[86] She hadn't been able to see herself in the art—to see herself *as* art.

* * *

For decades, fashion was the only avant-garde thing the USA could not steal from Europe. The French government would not let Americans have it. After World War II, France aggressively supported an industry and marketing empire around the 1950s ultrafeminine, luxe, declaredly anti-war New Look, which flowed from the powerful House of Dior from 1947 onwards. Throughout the 20th century, Paris remained the world's fashion capital, Marshall Plan be damned. To this day, only the French Ministry of Industry can approve the use of the term *haute couture*, which has nationalist, technical, legal, and commercial implications.

By the 1990s, however, New York's profanity made a sea change. Through the 1970s and 1980s, designers such as Gloria Vanderbilt, Diane von Furstenberg, Ralph Lauren, Calvin Klein, and more had accelerated ready-to-wear *couture* into mass-market American business. The shift is decisive in *Sex and the City*, the Emmy-winning TV series that debuted in 1998 and depicted four affluent white women navigating the complicated frontier of casual sex in New York. The characters were foul-mouthed, horny, heavy-drinking, and selfish, doing it all while slipping in and out of runway looks. It was a far cry from the cinched-waist, mannequin-virginity of the New Look, although Paris was a fantasy for the show's lead character Carrie Bradshaw (Sarah Jessica Parker), who chain-smoked, had affairs, and tromped on cobblestones in heels like her Parisian idols, yet never really bothered to learn a word of proper French.

In season three, episode 17, Carrie wears one of her many now-iconic outfits, the Fall-Winter 2000 John Galliano for Christian Dior newspaper-print slip dress. The dress is a centrepiece of postmodern art. It references the Italian-born Paris-based fashion designer Elsa Schiaparelli, an admirer of and collaborator with the Surrealists. Schiaparelli began making clothing with newspaper prints in the 1930s. Her inspirations riffed on the avant-garde Duchamp had built. A fan of shock, Schiaparelli popularized and branded a particular hue of fuchsia pink she called "Shocking Pink," later naming her signature *parfum* "Shocking de Schiaparelli" and titling her memoir *Shocking Life*. Her idea for newspaper-print clothing, she told *Harper's Bazaar* in 1935, came from a trip to Copenhagen, where she saw old women fishmongers sitting "for hours on the banks of the canals amidst waves of silver-scaled fish that were still alive and shimmering. These women wore on their heads newspapers twisted into queer shapes of hats."[87] On arriving home, Schiaparelli clipped newspaper articles about herself, "both complementary and otherwise, in every sort of language, stuck them together like a puzzle, and had them printed on silk and cotton."[88]

Galliano is one of fashion's many bad boys. His first runway show was inspired by the French Revolution, his Fall-Winter 1998 collection titled "A Voyage on the Diorient Express, or the Story of the Princess Pocahontas." A bizarre anti-Semitic tirade had him suspended from Dior in 2011. Galliano's own newspaper-print slip dress was a branding extravaganza for the House of Dior, under his name. Unlike Schiaparelli's, however, Galliano's collage was fake. The newspaper he "clipped" was the fabricated "Christian Dior Daily," emblazoned across the dress's waist. Other concocted headlines celebrated Galliano's genius and values: "Le plus important, c'est la curiosité"; "Il ose nous faire rêver"; "Mon rôle est de séduire." Above the Dior masthead: "Business: Dior Sales Up," and "Men's Fashion: Sex and the Cybermale—A Special Report." Like Schiaparelli, Galliano evoked class profanity with his newspaper print, part of a collection of "hobo-chic" clothing inspired by New York's early 20th-century aristocratic "Tramp Balls" and the homeless Galliano saw on late-night and early-morning Parisian streets, wrapped in newspaper to keep warm. (The whole thing was parodied in *Zoolander* the next year.)

At the beginning of "What Goes Around Comes Around," that *Sex and the City* episode, Carrie is mugged at gunpoint in Soho, a surprise in Mayor Rudy Giuliani's spruced-up New York. The mugger takes Carrie's Fendi bag ("it's a baguette," she corrects[89]) and her Manolo Blahnik strappy sandals. "These guys weren't just after money anymore," Carrie says, in voiceover. "They were after *fashion*."[90]

True to its title, the episode's theme is relationship karma. "Does everything that goes around *really* come around," Carrie asks, in voiceover, "and if so, will it come around to bite you in the ass?"[91] She could be talking about the Nietzschean-Groysian new. When Carrie hears a rumour that the married man she's fucking is now separated, she goes to a restaurant to confront his wife with a poorly thought-out apology, wearing the Dior newspaper-print dress. The furious wife dresses her down. The Dior dresses her up. In the episode's ultimate moment, fresh from the encounter, Carrie walks slow-motion down a crowded Manhattan street. Socially disgraced and sexually magnetic, she is literally front-page news.

* * *

It is well known that the history of the Internet traces back to Cold War-era US statecraft. Less discussed is how early Information Age innovations, fortifications on a geopolitical level, became fortifications on a personal level.

In 1953, Alex F. Osborn, the US advertising executive and putative inventor of brainstorming,[92] published *Applied Imagination: Principles and Procedures of Creative Problem-Solving*. The dust jacket of my 1963 edition boasts that it is the nineteenth printing and third revised edition, having sold more than 150,000 copies. Under the subtitle, a quote from Einstein: "Imagination is more important than knowledge." Inside, assertions that would not be out of place in Barnett Newman's writings, such as "Imagination is as universal as memory."[93] Referring to the Cuban Missile Crisis of the previous year, Osborn's updated introduction opines that, had the US government "been geared for idea-production, we might have been able to throw Castro's bomb right back."[94] The US imagination is suffocated by morality, Osborn claims. Whereas:

> The Soviet leaders are free to fabricate big lies at any time and quickly put them into orbit. The least our government could do would be to conduct a pilot-type of experiment—a six-month's try-out of a panel of able ideators whose only duty would be to think up ideas—just as the only duty of many scientists is to think up missiles.[95]

How did the West get from Osborn to, say, Richard Florida? Reckwitz proposes three, consecutive 20th-century regimes of novelty: modernity as perfection, modernity as progress, and aesthetic modernity.[96] In the first, early modernism by another name, the new is complete—a means by which to end any old structures not in step with industrial values.[97] Here, the new is aspirational, utopian, even totalitarian: a portal into a static, "perfect" future. In the second regime, novelty is the new reality. It is produced *ad infinitum*, with the demand for improvement in science, technology, and economy the new normal.[98] In the third regime, the contemporary West, genuine novelty is not of interest.[99] The future imagined by the first regime has arrived, the ideal of the second practically impossible. The new is now sensory movement from one stimulus to another: "the interesting, the surprising, and the original"—the "*relatively* new event."[100] For Reckwitz, echoing Horkheimer and Adorno, this regime is about information in the form of factoids, ideas, rumours, instructions, preferences, more—thin communication. Information possesses the required *minimum* of novelty. Digital society, running on infinite networks of information, is the ultimate work of mechanical art.

Osborn's emphasis on the Cold War as impetus for the application of imagination starts where Guilbaut leaves off, the historical bridge from the second to the third regime. Indeed, what Osborn called for was already happening. Project RAND ("research and development") began in 1945 at the Hamilton Army Airfield in Marin County, California.[101] It later became the RAND Corporation, headquartered on a beach in Santa Monica and supported through a loan from the recently established Ford Foundation[102]—which would go on to receive rumoured billions from the CIA for its liberal-imperialist projects across the globe.[103] Also in 1945, US engineer and Washington war strategist Vannevar Bush published his famous article in the *Atlantic Monthly* arguing that, while there may be no substitute for creative thought, it is aided by repetitive thought, for which "there are, and may be, powerful mechanical aids."[104] Bush dreamed up his "memex," a mechanized supplement to the human memory that foretells of the personal computer and AI. Here, positive change is positive thought—and must be multiplied on a more-than-human scale.

US scholar Pamela M. Lee notes that "operations research," a combination of mathematics and computers with an emphasis on decision and strategy, had contributed to the Allied victory, so after the war there was an urgency to perpetuate such planning.[105] RAND's early-years mission to reverse Communism's advance was purposefully limitless, to make it competitive. The approach included aesthetics. Lee cites Sharon Ghamari-Tabrizi, who calls the RAND Corporation a "Cold War avant-garde" in her biography of Herman Kahn—

one of RAND's premiere military and economic strategists, who used cybernetics, games theory, and systems theory to speculate and strategize, and was an inspiration for the Dr. Strangelove character in US director Stanley Kubrick's titular 1964 film.[106]

In 1963, a RAND document looked back at its 15-year history to celebrate how, at the corporation, there was "a deliberate attempt to keep the atmosphere at RAND informal and unrestrictive, to provide a climate suitable for creative work."[107] According to one participant, RAND was a "superb" team of people but also "more than a collection of people; it is a social organism characterized by intellect, imagination, and good humour."[108] Lee depicts an emerging neoliberal order: nimble, liquid, deregulated, both specialized and integrated. She also depicts a way of being and knowledge-sharing that rejects any form of destabilization by nature. A 1959 *LIFE* magazine article would, Lee notes, introduce RAND to the world, calling its intellectuals a "valuable bunch of brains."[109] In their 1994 manifesto titled "Cyberspace and the American Dream: A Magna Carta for the Knowledge Age," Esther Dyson, George Gilder, George Keyworth, and Alvin Toffler would similarly proclaim that "the central event of the 20th century is the overthrow of matter" and, in an echo not just of RAND but of Bacon, that "the powers of mind are everywhere ascendant over the brute force of things."[110]

The US art world responded to RAND and its ilk. "Systems aesthetics" appeared years after the think tank's inauguration but was intrinsically linked to the Silicon Valley innovators for whom Dyson et al. spoke. Systems aesthetics was inspired by the theories of mathematician Norbert Wiener, whose *Cybernetics: Or Control and Communication in the Animal and the Machine* was published in 1948.[111] In the September 1968 issue of *Artforum*, the critic and theorist Jack Burnham, who would join the German artist Hans Haacke at the Massachusetts Institute of Technology (MIT) in short order, published his own manifesto "Systems Esthetics."[112] In it, Burnham turns from any clear affiliation with politics or morality, a stance similar to the Abstract Expressionists, whom Burnham disavows, and to the aforementioned libertarian hippies who founded Silicon Valley.

Systems aesthetics did not want a bombastic entrance. According to Burnham, citing Kuhn, the movement was a "morphological development" and paradigm shift. Burnham also cites the US economist John Kenneth Galbraith, whom Burnham notes fits neither left nor right. What is necessary, according to Galbraith's *New Industrial State*, is an "evolving technostructure"[113] on which think tanks were already working, and in which there is a meditation on the role of the so-called technocracy. Burnham criticizes the current yet old-fashioned attachment to "new," comparing cars to modern art, where visual changes are deemed sufficient but do nothing to advance anything. The needs of now, Burnham writes, include:

> maintaining the biological livability of the Earth, producing more accurate models of social interaction, understanding the growing symbiosis in man machine relationships, establishing priorities for the usage and conservation of natural resources, and defining alternate patterns of education, productivity, and leisure.[114]

Relationships between the organic and non-organic must achieve stability. They might do this using systems analysis, which, notes Burnham, after Galbraith, involves aesthetic criteria. Systems analysis has application far beyond warfare. Alas, governments who do not understand this are in the ironic position of depriving their citizens of the tools they need to survive destruction.

The "aesthetics" of systems aesthetics often took the form of stark environments, in which ideas were subject to field testing, and art audiences and control groups merged. Burnham praises a "recent environment" by artist Les Levine that sounds like a torture chamber:

> rows of live electric wires emitted small shocks to passersby. Here behaviour is controlled in an esthetic situation with no primary reference to visual circumstances. As Levine insists, "What I am after here is physical reaction, not visual concern."[115]

Systems aesthetics' big moment came with Trinidadian-US curator Kynaston McShine's 1970 show at MoMA titled *Information*, the design concept of which seemed to anticipate the offices of a contemporary start-up, all-white with bean-bag chairs, its interactive art surveilling the sociopolitical opinions of its attendees. Haacke presented a *MoMA Poll* asking attendees if they would be less likely to re-elect New York Governor Nelson A. Rockefeller, then-trustee and former president of MoMA, if he continued to refuse to denounce the US military's Cambodian campaign. (The foundation of Rockefeller's own family was, like the Ford Foundation, strongly rumoured to have CIA ties.) Ballots were placed in Plexiglas boxes for viewers to see the results. Argentine collective Group Frontera's work videotaped visitors answering questions such as "How do you define power?" and "Could you be friends with a homosexual?" The footage was played on monitors in a nearby gallery.[116]

When Staniszewski observes that the "Information" artists were conceptualists who were also "artist worker[s]" and "cultural producers," that they "wrote texts as would critics, installed shows as would curators, printed publications as would publishers, and sold and distributed their work as would dealers,"[117] hindsight considers not just DIY gumption but today's burnt-out culture workers. As Staniszewski notes, however, "Information" was not a new venture for the laboratory of MoMA. It combined aesthetics and politics, and celebrated an anonymized citizen-viewer.[118] Even MoMA's 1934 *Machine Art* show had a poll in which audience members, alongside celebrity judges such as Amelia Earhart, voted on their favourite works.[119]

It is worth considering the contributions of two figures whom McShine acknowledges as influential in his curatorial essay for *Information*:[120] the US musician John Cage and the Canadian media theorist Marshall McLuhan. Cage's role in the art world would constantly be deemed new, his interdisciplinary approach essential to understanding how information and aesthetics increasingly merged in the mid-20th century to create a template for imaginative being. McLuhan would go on to praise proto-Information Age types like Cage, McLuhan's phrases providing a lexicon for the US counterculture that, raised in the shadow of nuclear war, wanted badly to mature into an anxiety-free future.

Cage, one of Tomkins's "bachelors," began his radical experiments long before systems aesthetics. Cage's impetus was Zen Buddhism: according to Tomkins, "purposeless play—simply to wake up to the very life we're living, which is so excellent once one gets one's mind and one's desires out of its way and lets it act of its own accord."[121] Cage was not to foresee a spiritual revolution, however. Rather, he would provide a template for the artist as creative programmer, with expression as data and music going "beyond chance... *there are no catastrophes.*"[122] Cage's most famous work, *4'33"*, places Benjamin's ideal of deep listening into the realm of classical music. The ultimate in avant-garde praxis, it is 4 minutes and 33 seconds of silence, meant to reveal the sounds that traditional performance conceals.

Cage's autistic manner and quirky personal style suggest the nerds that would later populate Silicon Valley. Indeed, Tomkins presents Cage as an accidental entrepreneur. A highlight of his book concerns Cage's appearance on an Italian quiz show, where Cage won the grand prize as a mycologist, or mushroom expert, and was nicknamed "the good-looking Frankenstein" by the Italian press, after his bushy buzzcut.[123] But Cage wasn't always endearing. He ran afoul of the musicians of the New York Philharmonic, who hissed their instruments at him and refused to play his scores, upon which "Cage spoke to their union representative."[124] "I am going toward violence rather than tenderness," Cage tells Tomkins at one point.[125]

Like Cage, McLuhan endeavoured to see art everywhere—and to embrace what he saw. Burnham quotes McLuhan's thoughts on Pop: "the entire environment was ready to become a work of art."[126] McLuhan's mid-1960s books *Understanding Media* and *The Medium is the Massage* were bestsellers, and, at the height of his popularity, McLuhan would self-abridge his complex theories, spouting soundbites and aphorisms on TV and in magazines, soon taken up by turned-on Western hippies. Most famously, McLuhan suggested electronic media were creating a "global village" causing humanity to adopt a more "tribal" attitude toward social life, mores, time, bureaucracy, more.[127] The song "Age of Aquarius" from the musical *Hair*—its subtitle, "The American Tribal Love-Rock Musical"—would not exist without McLuhan.

But McLuhan was no utopianist. In 1968's *War and Peace in the Global Village*, he recounts the "now" with oracular dread. Quoting US biologist Otto Lowenstein, McLuhan augurs Reckwitz: the new causes shock and disorientation. At first sight, the new is meaningless and confounding. Then, quickly, it has its own imperatives, which destabilize everyone except the artist, implying that, in turn, everyone will be forced to become an artist:

> Today, electronics and automation make mandatory that everybody adjust to the vast global environment as if it were his little home town. The artist is the only person who does not shrink from this challenge... He glories in the invention of new identities, corporate and private, that for the political and educational establishments... bring anarchy and despair.[128]

McLuhan became melancholy by the early 1970s. Increasingly resigned to the social turmoil around him, he struggled with his role as educator at the University of Toronto, which, like other universities at the time, was corporatizing, a trend forged by Stanford, hub of systems analysts and future tech moguls, and property owner of a significant portion of what would become Silicon Valley. McLuhan may have said to *Playboy* in 1969 that "we're standing on the threshold of a liberating and exhilarating world" but, in his private life, informed by his abiding Catholicism and his sometimes-troubled children, he came to feel the opposite.[129]

McLuhan's ideas and persona would take the think tanks of RAND into popular culture as "futurology"—a phenomenon of the 1960s and 1970s in which various interdisciplinary experts held forth about what was to come. Toffler, co-author of that 1994 cyber manifesto, was the US's pre-eminent futurologist, in all senses a poor man's McLuhan. Toffler's essay "The Future as a Way of Life" had appeared in *Horizon* magazine in 1965, and his bestselling *Future Shock* was on the cusp of being released when Burnham wrote his own manifesto. Toffler's observations are inelegant and prolix. One reviewer called *Future Shock* "a high-school term paper gone berserk."[130] Toffler's future is not determined but *terra nullius*, waiting to be filled with a million ideas. Futurology, argues Swedish-French scholar Jenny Andersson, is a type of knowledge production—a means of stimulating the imagination, of making the future rather than predicting it.[131] (There are still futurologists in Western culture. Israeli historian Yuval Noah Harari's bestselling 2015 book *Homo Deus: A Brief History of Tomorrow*, a follow-up to his bestselling *Sapiens: A Brief History of Humankind*, asks questions such as, "Who might inherit humankind, and what new religion might replace humanism?"[132])

Toffler influenced those who birthed the personal computer. Regis McKenna, Apple's first marketing guru, claimed to have read him repeatedly.[133] Particularly influential was *Future Shock*'s celebration of nomadism—a symptom of growing US innovation whose wandering spirit offers a form of emotional protection. Toffler quotes an airline executive who avoids political involvement because "in a few years I won't even be living here. You plant a tree and you never see it grow."[134] Toffler goes on to criticize the concept of home, which, after the Industrial Revolution, received, in his words, "syrupy glorification" in Victorian culture.[135] Silicon Valley prophet Stewart Brand, publisher of *The Whole Earth Catalog*, would in turn fetishize nomadic Indigenous nations and cowboys alike. (The *Catalog*, a sort of *Sears* catalog for back-to-the-landers, featured "tools" for subsistence and self-sufficiency, and carried buckskin jackets in its "Industry and Craft" section.) In his well-known study of Brand, Fred Turner notes parallel comments by John Perry Barlow, Grateful Dead lyricist and info-tech journalist, and by Esther Dyson, also an info-tech journalist. Barlow, who had penned his own "Declaration of the Independence of Cyberspace," claimed in the 1990s that he lived only at "barlow@eff.org." Dyson, in her 1997 guide *Release 2.0: A Design for Living in the Digital Age*, claimed her only fixed address was "on the Net."[136] It should not be surprising that both Barlow and Dyson come from affluent families.

Future Shock has much in common with two "shock" titles published decades later: Naomi Klein's *The Shock Doctrine* (2007), about the neoliberal statecraft that emerged from the Chicago School of Economics, particularly the economist Milton Friedman, and Robert Hughes's *The Shock of the New: Art and the Century of Change* (1980), about the history of the Western avant-garde. Klein's pivotal quote from Friedman is about crisis: "Only a crisis—actual or perceived—produces real change. When that crisis occurs, the actions that are taken depend on the ideas that are lying around."[137] Friedman's "ideas that are lying around" are not quite the same as the newspaper clippings on the floor of Elsa Schiaparelli's 1930s Paris studio. Thatcher's divide-and-conquer strategy is not quite the same as Hughes's description of the art movement Fauvism, which emerged alongside Futurism—"an all-out assault on the senses."[138] Yet, all three authors depict a West in which the future depends on a kind of perpetual change that has little to do with anything new, and everything to do with the promise of it.

In her 2010 book *Blog Theory*, US political theorist Jodi Dean argues that digital society is a form of so-called communicative capitalism, which captures ideas, insights, critiques, and more, but ensures they do not become a bigger theory that contributes to meaningful critique of, and political resistance to, the present state of things.[139] In the West, information is circulated but never formed. It is also captured, reflected in big-data mining and surveillance—contemporary ways of life. Communication, that needful human thing, is now both a resource and a shield from weakness. But we are far from deluded, Dean argues. Because we are in dizzying realms of shifting information, we *desire* friction-free relationships. It's just easier that way.

Still, there is a type of newness that leftist "techno-enthusiasts" claim is a more sustainable alternative.[140] Dean cites author Steve Johnson's theories on "emergent behaviour":[141] forms of self-organization, often modeled after the natural world but also found in software, favouring decentralization and bottom-up thinking. Crisis will occur, but can be eased by feedback. Johnson praises the concept of homeostasis, long beloved of systems theorists, where crisis reaches a point of auto-generated stability, equilibrium, continuity—solutions not unlike the promises of free-market capitalism. What emergence does not account for, Dean argues, is the wealth of information in physical interaction. Johnson praises humans for being able to assess, even predict, what others' mental states are. But this is not in fact natural. In real life, minds and dispositions change. Rich human insight comes through bodies, moving and communicating together, in shared states of uncertainty.

* * *

Dean uses the term "displaced mediators" to describe people like Stewart Brand, who "[trigger] a process of change even as change quickly overtakes [them]."[142] Brand and the so-called New Communalists, of which he was a part, were displaced mediators when they modified the military's experiments with their own left-libertarian refusal, eventually turning into the group that developed the early Internet. Yet, the New Communalist promise of free circulation of ideas and tools, including software, ended up producing inequality and anxiety. What started as a vehicle for the new became a means by which to further entrench the old, "now strengthened by the rhetoric of its own over-coming."[143]

As with Herbert Bayer at the MoMA, Brand wanted to provide a 360-degree field of vision. He wanted everyone to see the world, all of it, at once. Brand's idol was Buckminster Fuller, grandnephew of Margaret Fuller, the 19th-century journalist, women's rights advocate, and frequenter of Brook Farm who had edited *The Dial*, where the transcendentalists were published. In *Ideas and Integrities* (1963), Buckminster Fuller imagined the "Comprehensive Designer," an interdisciplinarian who would not have institutional affiliation but instead be "a harvester of the potential of the realm."[144] The Comprehensive Designer would reap ideas lying around, seeing both macrocosm and microcosm. (Fuller's patented geodesic dome, a 1960s and 1970s image of sustainable living, resembled a bubble, a honeycomb, the earth itself. The domes fell out of fashion once anyone who built them tried to weather a rainy season and discovered that they reliably leak.) A futurologist, the Comprehensive Designer would not change the world through top-down hierarchy and industry, but bottom-up interdisciplinary design science.[145] Fuller himself migrated from university to university the way Silicon Valley's innovators would migrate from start-up to start-up because of the unenforceability of noncompete clauses in California. Like these innovators, Fuller would not draw a direct line to all his forbears. "A quick glance back at MIT's Rad Lab in World War II," Turner writes, "would have reminded Fuller's audiences that interdisciplinary migration and multi-institutional collaboration were key features of the military research world."[146]

The LSD- and psilocybin-occasioned parties that are part of 1960s and 1970s lore were Fullerian. LSD had its own institutionalized history, and Brand took his first acid trip in 1962 at the International Federation for Advanced Study, co-founded by an Ampex engineer and a Stanford engineer professor. His dose was given to him by Jim Fadiman, also affiliated with Stanford.[147] Four years later, Brand sat shivering in a blanket on a San Francisco roof, tripping again, seeing the curve of the earth and thinking about Fuller's idea that people have internalized the world as flat, and thereby see its resources as unlimited. He told Turner:

> There were no public photographs of the whole earth at that time despite the fact that we were in the space program for about ten years. I started scheming within the trip. How can I make this photograph happen? Because I have now persuaded myself that it will change everything if we have this photograph looking at the earth from space.[148]

In his journal, Brand wrote, "Why Haven't We Seen a Photograph of the Whole Earth Yet?" and, underneath this, "Whole New World."

The result of Brand's acid-trip epiphany overlaid art, commerce, expression, information, and identity. He began to sell buttons with his acid-trip question printed on them—at Berkeley, then across the country at college campuses. While peddling his wares, he wore a top hat with a flower in it and a sandwich board with the question from his journal on it. According to a 1966 *Village Voice* article, a young woman at Columbia University asked Brand what would happen "if we did have a picture"—"Would it eliminate slums, or meanness, or anything?" "Maybe not," Brand responded, "but it might tell us something about ourselves." "What?" she asked. "It might tell us where we're at," he answered. "What for?" she asked. "Why do you look in the mirror?" he replied. The *Voice* reported that the young woman bought a button.[149]

The first *Whole Earth Catalog* was published in Fall 1968, a year after NASA released its first picture of the whole earth, and the same year the Apollo 8 crew released the "earthrise" photo from the moon, which would appear on subsequent issues of the *Catalog*. Later, in the 1970s, a straight-on "blue-marble" image of earth, a version of which appeared on the first *Whole*

Earth Catalog, would be mass-marketed on posters, T-shirts, and more. Journalists have credited the image for prompting the environmental movement. The mission statement in the first *Whole Earth Catalog* read as follows:

> We are as gods and might as well get good at it. So far, remotely done power and glory—as via government, big business, formal education, church—has succeeded to the point where gross defects obscure actual gains. In response to this dilemma and to these gains a realm of intimate, personal power is developing—power of the individual to conduct his own education, find his own inspiration, shape his own environment, and share his adventure with whoever is interested. Tools that aid this process are sought and promoted by the WHOLE EARTH CATALOG.[150]

On June 21, 1971, Brand threw a "demise party" for the *Whole Earth Catalog* to celebrate its final issue. Brand had been part of the systems aesthetics scene in New York, had spent time with author Ken Kesey and his group the Merry Pranksters, and so was no stranger to happenings and performance art. The demise party was held at the new Exploratorium at San Francisco's Palace of Fine Arts, a surreal, kitschy, neoclassical complex surrounded by a lagoon, built for the 1915 Panama-Pacific International Exposition. Bernard R. Maybeck, its architect, had intended for the structure simply to fall into ruin after the exposition and by the mid-1960s it was being torn down and rebuilt—a project ongoing by the time of Brand's party. In 1969, the physicist Frank Oppenheimer, who, with his brother J. Robert Oppenheimer, worked on the Manhattan Project that produced the world's first nuclear weapons, opened the Exploratorium in-process, its installations on view to a public that was invited to participate in their development.[151]

The demise party was described by local Bay Area news as "a bizarre countercultural Yippee demonstration on the pointlessness of money."[152] Barefoot and dressed in a black monk's cassock, Brand stood before the 500-person crowd and promised them a "surprise educational event." After a procession and entertainment, including clowns and belly dancers, master of ceremonies Scott Beach approached the microphone to announce that Brand had just given him $20,000 in $100 bills. "He gave it to the people here to be used as a tool... as a seed," Beach announced. "The *Whole Earth Catalog* ceases. The seeds have been planted already. Your consensus will decide what will be done with this money."[153]

Suggestions during the evening, written on a blackboard, included burning the money and turning the debate into a game, in which the money was split and divided among subgroups. Several suggestions included giving the money to Indigenous communities. "The only responsibility we have as children of white middle-class America is to the people we ripped off," said Paul Krassner, *Whole Earth* contributor and editor.[154] "We need to find what can get us to all feel right about doing a thing," Brand said to the crowd. "It's not to the exclusion of anything else. It's just where we're going to plant this particular seed."[155] $5000 had disappeared among the crowd over the course of the evening, and ultimately the crowd voted on giving the money to one Frederick L. Moore, who would put the money in the bank and throw another party to decide what to do with it. As Turner relates, what became of the money is unclear, although Moore went on, four years later, to co-found the Homebrew Computer Club, famed incubator for Silicon Valley entrepreneurs Steve Jobs, co-founder of Apple, and Bill Gates, co-founder of Microsoft.[156]

In 1967, the French writer Jean-Jacques Servan-Schreiber published *Le Défi Américain*, about the failure of Europe to keep pace with the USA's research-and-development prowess, and the need for Europe to invest not just in science but in US-style management and marketing methods.[157] As Margaret O'Mara notes in *The Code: Silicon Valley and the Remaking of America*, Silicon Valley, which grew from Stanford-connected innovators and its next-door companies, was a site of aggressive calls for deregulation from the beginning. In the 1950s, at a time of widespread unionization, Hewlett Packard emphasized its own environment as a place of non-traditional worker sport—its employees played volleyball and horseshoes out on the lawn—and boosted employee loyalty through stock options.[158] David Packard would go on to become a vocal critic of the welfare state. Indeed, O'Mara suggests that, with the industry building around the silicon transistor, a model for Silicon Valley success was taking place: grow through venture capitalists, give non-organized employees stock options in lieu of benefits and pensions, and disrupt, disrupt, disrupt.

The epigraph of the third chapter of O'Mara's book comes from the 1962 Jimmy Stewart Western *The Man Who Shot Liberty Valance*: "This is the West, sir. When legend becomes fact, print the legend."[159] That Apple printed the legend is well-known. Apple would invoke British natural philosopher Isaac Newton and British Romantic poet William Wordsworth in its ads. In 1984, its Superbowl commercial was made by British director Ridley Scott, fresh off his sci-fi film *Bladerunner*. It showed a white, female track-and-field athlete—the only thing in colour in the ad—running through a crowd of shaved-head drones and throwing an industrial hammer into a large screen broadcasting their leader. "On January 24th," said the voiceover, "Apple Computer will introduce Macintosh. And you'll see why 1984 won't be like *1984*."[160] But the result of the athlete's disruption is unclear. During the voiceover, the camera pans the audience, who have not been enlivened by the runner's act. Now slack-jawed, they resemble the non-playable characters (NPCs) of videogames, current symbols of the alt-right's disdain for left-liberal orthodoxy. They could also resemble Bayer's everyviewer. Scott's aesthetic, a shameless quotation of Nazi filmmaker Leni Riefenstahl, gives the lie to the commercial's ambitiously written copy. In hindsight, the copy and the imagery match perfectly.

* * *

Close to the Machine: Technophilia and Its Discontents is a 1997 memoir-cum-novel by computer programmer and tech columnist Ellen Ullman, published by San Francisco's Beat publisher City Lights and blurbed by Brand who, by 1997, was an architect of internet culture: the *Catalog* had become the Whole Earth 'Lectronic Link (WELL), a teleconferencing system via a central computer that, in real time and asynchronously, connected users in a social network beginning in 1985.[161] "Computer programmers are remaking the world," wrote Brand of Ullman's book. "Here is ground truth about that world-making and brilliant critique of it. The reader vibrates between delight and alarm on every page."[162]

Brand is correct. "I have no idea what time it is," Ullman begins. She is in a windowless office programming with a guy named Joel. They've been there for days, trying to get rid of a bug in the software.[163] Ullman can't recall for the reader the company for whom she is working. The real world has fallen away; it's just about the bug. After having successfully debugged, Ullman and Joel part. She hopes she doesn't see him again. If she does, the bug is back.

Ullman is a veteran computer programmer in her 40s but rarely feels like an expert. In computer work, there is constant change and "[t]he corollary of constant change is ignorance."[164] Ullman also works for the City of San Francisco, where she creates a registration-system network for people with HIV/AIDS. As a sometime civil servant, she thinks of herself as a bad techie. (Most techies, she notes, are libertarians). She also worries she's a bad activist. The network is named "Jerry," after a Black activist in the community. But the system is not Jerry. Many users it is meant to serve can't access it because they don't own a computer. The director of the project wants to check the data Jerry collects against a larger database, to ensure providers are compliant with contracts and funding sources. The whole point, Ullman notes, was the program's gentler non-compliance. The director disagrees: "the people paying for this system have the right to good data."[165]

Ullman casually dates Brian, a "cypherpunk" hacker and self-described "anarchocapitalist" deeply into crypto, already a thing in the 1990s. Brian is 31, wears baggy jeans and a motorcycle jacket, has long hair, a short, pointy beard, and is rarely seen without a cowboy hat. He makes Ullman feel like a "figment of his sexual imagination."[166] They talk in a sushi restaurant and then at Ullman's home, where she tries to woo him by playing him British composer Thomas Tallis's 16th-century choral masterpiece *Spem in alium*, even though he's just told her that "classical music is not yet in my databanks."[167] Brian goes on, as if to himself, about setting up his crypto business "extralegally... at the very heart of money."[168] The two have "tantric, algorithmic" sex.[169] "He has been with himself too long," Ullman writes.[170] She considers their robotic pillow talk the next day, where Brian tells her the new breed of entrepreneur is "Net landlord."[171]

Ullman wanders in and out of connection, disconnection. Her job is her life:

> My work hours have leaked into all parts of the day and week. Eight in the morning, ten at night, Saturday at noon, Sundays: I am never not working. Even when I'm not actually doing something that could be called work, I might get started any minute. So everything is an interruption—a

call from a friend, an invitation to lunch—everything must be refused because it is possible that from one moment to the next I will get back to something.[172]

Ullman tries to hold onto a book of code from earlier in her career—a souvenir of her accomplishments. Brian tells her to toss it but to keep the cover, an aesthetic relic. "I'm watching the great, spinning, cutting edge slice away from me—and I'm just watching," Ullman writes. "I'm almost fascinated by my own self-destructiveness... This terrifies me. It also makes me feel buoyant and light."[173]

In 1997, I had not heard of Ullman. I rarely used a computer, and it would be years before I could connect to the Internet at home. I was an English Lit major in Winnipeg who listened to a lot of indie rock from the USA. Some of it was released on the Arlington, Virginia-based label Simple Machines, run by Jenny Toomey and Kristin Thomson, who had their own band called Tsunami.

The indie rock scene at the time was, as is well-known, resolutely DIY. Labels had basic websites and well-designed mail-order catalogs, with reasonably priced and often limited-edition CDs, LPs, and 7-inch singles. Indie tactility was a reaction against the mega-corporate 1980s, and also the Internet, which seemed to threaten the very world of the handmade. "An American lives in anticipation of the future," Ronald Reagan said in 1979, "because he knows it will be a great place."[174] 1990s indie rock resisted this. It also had its own, exclusive social networks, which challenge any recollection of the movement as subversive.

Tsunami's "Kidding on the Square," one of the Simple Machines 7-inches, was part of a year-long project in 1993 for which the label released a two-band 7-inch every month, in the manner of a musical calendar. The project was called "Working Holiday," each 7-inch celebrating a holiday or historical event in the month in which it was released. According to Simple Machines's website, it was "a year's worth of stuffing, stamping, boxing, and shipping 36,000 7-inches"—hard work, with small returns. In "Kidding on the Square," Toomey, a sharp, intellectual songwriter with a powerful voice, delivers an internal monologue that tells her own story of that year. Some guy says she "smells like cardboard." She should know "coffee isn't food." She promises herself she'll stay up all night to meet a deadline but never does—"in the morning, there'll be mail to do." She's not a radical, she sings to herself. "You're just a cold old square with dark circles under her eyes."[175]

Toomey would beat a path from DIY to tech-policy professional. She is now an employee of the Ford Foundation, having helmed its International Technology and Society Team and its US Internet Freedom Team. 1990s indie rockers would call this selling out. But Toomey's former career was not sustainable. In "Kidding on the Square," she is the threadbare, alt version of Ullman's overworked, disaffected Silicon Valley programmer. At the song's end, Toomey asks herself if she has the strength, then the guts, to "pick up a penny... off the ground."[176] And with one sickly, off-tune guitar chord, the song burns out with her.

Epilogue
Deeper Understanding

The first sound anyone heard on a Kate Bush album was a whale song, at the start of "Moving," track one on 1978's *The Kick Inside*.[1] Put another way, the first sound anyone heard on a Kate Bush album was a sample of a recording made by Frank Watlington, a US naval engineer who accidentally heard whale songs while listening for Soviet submarines off the coast of Bermuda with an underwater microphone.[2] Put another way, the first sound anyone heard on a Kate Bush album was a sample of the song "Slowed Down Solo Whale," itself a sample of the recording by Watlington and released on what remains one of the best-selling nature albums of all time, *Songs of the Humpback Whale* (1970), produced and arranged by US zoologist and bio-acoustician Roger Payne.[3] Put another way, the first sound anyone heard on a Kate Bush album was the vocalization of nonhuman mammals declaring fitness—wanting, as has been widely presumed but still not fully understood, to connect, to fuck.

The first sound anyone hears on "Deeper Understanding," the sixth song on Kate Bush's 1989 album *The Sensual World*, is Bush's own voice, immediately: "As the people here turn colder / I turn to my computer / And spend my evenings with it / Like a friend." The vagaries of Bush's introduction—who is "I" and where is "here"?—are soon grounded in period technology: "I was loading a new program / I had ordered from a magazine."[4]

"Deeper Understanding" is related by an isolated narrator, ground down by the detachment of contemporary life. Unable to relate with others, the narrator becomes obsessed with an AI-like mail-ordered computer program designed to keep its user company. The computer intimately appreciates and replies to the narrator, the song's chorus being the computer's voice: "Hello, I know that you're unhappy / I bring you love, a deeper understanding." Soon, satisfaction can't come from anything else. "I've never felt such pleasure," the narrator confesses. "Nothing else seemed to matter / I neglected my bodily needs."[5]

Decades after its release, Bush's song about a person falling in love with their computer feels both retro-kitsch and relatable. ("This song about Kate installing a program from a cd rom <3," texted one of my friends to me when Bush's remasters were released in late 2018.) In the first and second verses, Bush appears to sing of the "execute" command, common to the incipient personal computer. In the first verse, the narrator presses "execute," a riff, perhaps, on the "return" or "enter" key, and/or the ".exe," or executable, extensions of program-installation software. In the second verse, the verb changes, with added context: "I pick up the phone and *go* execute." This may conjure early network dial-up connections that culminated in the Internet, not yet commonplace at the time of "Deeper Understanding"'s release. It also suggests something darker: "go execute" means Bush's narrator is executing socially, cutting themselves off from family and friends attempting to "intervene" in the narrator's compulsive new relationship. (Of course, "execute" in computer programming contains only one of the word's English meanings, to carry out, and not the other, to carry out the killing of someone condemned to death.)

Bush's song has no resolution. The fate of her narrator is unclear, although there are sounds at the end seemingly meant to be organic, soothing: Bulgarian folk singing and, finally, birds chirping. A window has been opened. Something has been set free.

By the time Bush redid "Deeper Understanding" for 2011's *Director's Cut*, for which she took songs from *The Sensual World* and its 1993 follow-up, *The Red Shoes*, and stripped them of their supposedly dated studio production, some critics began (ironically, given *Director's Cut*'s impetus) to point to "Deeper Understanding"—mail-ordered program, voice console, and all—as prescient. "Kate Bush Invents the Internet with 'Deeper Understanding,'" reads a headline for an April 2015 *AV Club* thinkpiece by Katie Rife.[6] Not just the Internet: with Bush's "tired" and "unhappy" character who uses their computer so much they "could not eat" and "could not sleep," Bush may have foreseen Internet Addiction Disorder, which, as of writing, is unrecognized by the World Health Organization, but Googled enough to have its own Wikipedia page.[7]

Bush herself does not feel her "lonely" and "lost" character is ruined by the end of the song. "I suppose I really liked the idea of deep, spiritual communication—deep love which should come from humans—coming from the last place you'd expect it to, the coldest piece of machinery," she said in an October 1989 interview with *Melody Maker*. She goes on:

> And yet I do feel there is a link. I do feel that, in some ways, computers could take us into a level of looking at ourselves that we've never seen before, because they could come in from outside all this... I think a lot of things in nature are almost program-based, and a lot of things that we do are very mechanical, so maybe somehow going right through a computer, almost so that you come out the other side—going through all that science—will take us to something very spiritual but very earthy.[8]

By 1989, Kate Bush was an international pop star, following up her successful *Hounds of Love* album with a work that subtly communicated her disintegrating relationship with Del Palmer, her musical collaborator and lover for over a decade. What is a song about a shut-in PC user doing on a break-up album? In promotional interviews for *The Sensual World*, Bush would repeat that "Deeper Understanding" is a song about "being killed by love."[9] Bush's own significant relationship with technology, notably during the feverish making of her 1982 album *The Dreaming*, makes "Deeper Understanding" not merely autobiographical, but among the most complex love songs she ever wrote.

* * *

There can be no single inventor of the Internet. Feminist accounts of internet history stress networks and communities, with no fixed origin. Practices of sewing, knitting, and weaving, for instance, in which lines come together, mutable by pattern, in a kind of binary code (knits and purls), create technology such as clothing and tapestries—arguably, early forms of computing.

Such practices also formed the basis of pre-Internet, pre-industrial relational networks. French weaver and merchant Joseph Marie Jacquard's 19th-century automation of the loom with a punch card is often deemed the first computer,[10] but long before Jacquard, there were the weavers who, it is surmised but impossible to confirm, put coded messages into their handiwork. Jacquard's invention made many of these workers obsolete. Those who protested this and other industrial machinery became history's first Luddites, a term that has origins in labour rights, and has become pejorative.[11]

In the West, pre-industrial relational networks are feminized, with degrees of paranoia. There are the Greek Fates and the Norse Norns, pictured as women holding threads or yarn that, when crossed, tell of future doom.[12] During the French Revolution, so-called tricoteuses knitted while watching guillotine executions. In Charles Dickens's *A Tale of Two Cities*, Madame Defarge knits the names of those destined for the guillotine in secret code. In Greco-Roman myth, Philomela weaves the story of her rape into a tapestry, identifying her brother-in-law rapist who has cut out her tongue. (In 2018, the US writer Katy Waldman published a piece in the *New Yorker* comparing the Philomela myth to the #MeToo movement.[13])

By the early 20th century, Western communications technology was firmly in male hands, with some women, enlisted by the military, being *called* computers. In *Broad Band: The Untold Story of the Women Who Made the Internet*, US author and musician Claire L. Evans tells the story of human "computers," later gendered in productivity units as "kilogirls": mathematicians and similarly trained professionals who crunched numbers as part of collective workforces that managed large sets of data.[14] ("Kilogirls" was a measure of how powerful such collective workforces, that is, supercomputers, were—a measure of literal bodies. Contemporary coding has a similarly gendered workforce.)

If Evans's book aims to celebrate these early "computers," it also tells of co-optation, even collusion. During World War II, the US military developed the top-secret Electronic Numerical Integrator and Computer (ENIAC), a room-sized supercomputer powered by a group of women known as the ENIAC Six: Frances Bilas, Betty Jean Jennings, Ruth Lichterman, Kathleen "Kay" McNulty, Elizabeth "Betty" Snyder, and Marlyn Wescoff. After the war ended, the computer was revealed to the public, described breathlessly by journalists as "a giant brain."[15] Unlike the *LIFE* piece about RAND that appeared decades later and described the think tank similarly, the focus here was on the machine, not the women who powered it. "The amount of work that had to be done before you could ever get to a machine that was really doing any thinking to me just staggered the mind. I found this very annoying," Betty Jean Jennings said decades later. "It was more than annoying," Evans writes. "It effectively erased her."[16]

What exactly were these women building? The ENIAC Six worked on classified military projects aiming, among other things, to refine and accelerate ballistics. Their professional achievements were not just the solution of some abstract physics problems. "When their imaginary shell hit the ground, the mathematical model kept going, driving it through the earth with the same velocity and speed as it had while shooting through the air," Evans writes, describing the faulty trajectory of one of the simulations the ENIAC Six worked on. "This made the calculation worse than useless. If they didn't find some way to stop the bullet, they'd embarrass themselves in front of eminent mathematicians, the army, and their employers."[17]

Here is the tension of Evans's book. Notwithstanding their achievements, the ENIAC Six were employees of the military industrial complex and wanted very much to please their bosses. Industrial or post-industrial technology—accretive, like pre-industrial technology, but also a product, an event, a launch—does not easily contain consoling social change. As a new tool, it may mean quality of life and increased productivity. As an ancient phenomenon, accelerated, it signals perpetual departure: one point after another of no return.

* * *

"We were working secretly for the military," begins "Experiment IV," a bonus track on Kate Bush's 1986 greatest-hits compilation *The Whole Story*. "Our experiment in sound was nearly ready to begin / We only know in theory what we are doing / Music made for pleasure, music made to thrill."[18]

Like "Deeper Understanding," "Experiment IV" comes from Bush's own imagination, although it could easily be mistaken as an adaptation of the experiences of the ENIAC Six. The musical technicians in "Experiment IV" believe they are creating a state-of-the-art experiment in sound, perhaps one designed to heal and inspire, until it is revealed, at a moment too late to turn back, that they have been building a death machine. "They told us all they wanted / Was a sound that could kill someone from a distance," the chorus goes. The technicians in Bush's song are placed in ambivalent relation to their Frankenstein's monster. As fleshed out in the song's video, directed by Bush, the technicians hold their noses and continue their experiment in sound, absolving themselves of responsibility as their work turns ethically questionable. "But that dream is your enemy," Bush sings. "We won't be there to snitch / I just pray that someone there can hit the switch."

"Experiment IV" and "Deeper Understanding" are both likely about the Fairlight Computer Musical Instrument, also known as the Fairlight CMI synthesizer. This large, expensive machine has been ascribed many firsts—a musical emblem of the new—including first visual-digital music sequencer (you could compose music on its cathode-ray-tube screen, writing notation with a light pen) and first digital sampler (you could hook up a microphone to the computer, record any sound, and then pitch-shift it on a keyboard).[19]

The Fairlight is best known for the ORCH5, aka the "orchestra hit," a sample from the "Infernal Dance of All the Subjects of Kastchei" section of Igor Stravinsky's *The Firebird* (1910): a dissonant, fortissimo chord that opens the section abruptly, shockingly.[20] The attention getting ORCH5 became a staple of 1980s and 1990s pop, dance, and rap music, so much so that it is now largely unnoticed by listeners, or understood as a banal marker of the time. It is not a coincidence that the Fairlight's best-known sound is a violent modernist blast. As a physical object, the machine unmistakably recalls military technology that, in the early 1980s, had only been seen in films—its sequencer suggesting ballistic patterning, its return, or execute functions, kinds of detonations.

In a 1980s Fairlight demonstration video with US producer Quincy Jones, the US jazz artist Herbie Hancock, an early adopter of the Fairlight (he used it to make his 1983 hit "Rockit"), anticipates the problems purist musicians might have with the synthesizer—including that, like Jacquard's loom, it would replace them—and tries a rebuttal:

> These instruments were designed for people to use... It's just another tool, the way an axe is a tool... A synthesizer can be a tool to really hurt people's ears and interfere with their lives... It can be a tool to make a really nice-sounding instrument that can really affect people in a positive way. And it all depends on the person that's using it.[21]

Bush's PSYOP technicians in "Experiment IV" capture, among other things, "the painful cries of mothers" and "a terrifying scream": "we recorded it and put it into our machine." For a 1986 lip-synched performance of "Experiment IV" on BBC1's *Wogan* talk show, Bush and her band donned lab coats in a seated recreation of the video concept. Shots of Bush at a wooden desk clearly show the logo of a bandmate's Fairlight CMI in the background.[22]

It has long been recognized that Bush was an early Fairlight aficionado. Peter Vogel, the Australian co-developer of the Fairlight, explains in an interview for *Vox* that the Fairlight and other synthesizers allowed musicians to "create the music you had in your head a lot more easily than if you had to sit down and learn to play instruments from scratch."[23]

Bush is a pianist, although Vogel's words apply to her in the sense that the Fairlight acted as both a cheat and an expansion. As with the headset microphone Bush developed with sound engineer Gordon "Gunji" Patterson for her 1979 live show Tour of Life so that she could dance and sing at the same time, the Fairlight was not killing any part of her but rather adding something—which her body by turns accepted and rejected.

In 1979, the year the Fairlight was officially launched, there were only three machines in the UK.[24] The musician Peter Gabriel, with whom Bush had had a creative relationship since starting out, co-owned a company called Syco Systems that imported electronic instruments, and he had his own personal machine, with Syco owning the other two. Bush learned of the Fairlight through Gabriel, according to Bush biographer Graeme Thomson, and rented one while recording her album *Never for Ever*.[25] Everyone in the studio took turns making noises to record and put into the Fairlight. "We created a huge mess in Abbey Road Studio Two," remembers John L. Walters, who co-programmed the machine during the sessions, "smashing glasses and sampling them, recording and saving the best-sounding noises as digital files in the Fairlight's memory."[26] These glass-breaking noises ended up on Bush's "Babooshka," the second single from *Never for Ever*.

"For someone who had struggled on her first two records to articulate her feelings through sound, discovering the Fairlight was like stumbling into an Aladdin's Cave of sonic possibilities, opening a door into a new world," writes Thomson.[27] He quotes Kevin Cann and Sean Mayes, authors of a 1988 book about Bush, who contend that the Fairlight allowed Bush to "layer sounds as she layers ideas."[28] "Now she could add anything—strings, waterfalls, sunbursts—during the writing process itself," writes Thomson.[29] Says Bush:

> As soon as I saw [the Fairlight] I knew I had to have one, and it was going to become a very important part of my work... What attracts me to the Fairlight is its ability to create very human, animal, emotional sounds that don't actually sound like a machine. I think in a way that's what I've been waiting for.[30]

Not a new world, then, but a key to a long-locked door.

The induction of the Fairlight into Bush's musical and recording personnel allowed her not only to express herself better, but also to work more independently. Since her teens, Bush, who grew up with two older brothers, had little choice but to collaborate with a large ensemble of male musicians. Rock music in the 1970s, including progressive or "prog" rock, a genre with which Bush is associated, was characterized by excessively long studio sessions, sometimes with a variety of professional "session musicians," almost uniformly male, being called on to contribute to multi-tracked recordings, produced impeccably, to showcase the technology through which music was listened to, including FM radio and hi-fi speakers. Bush's brother John had taken her demos to David Gilmour of the band Pink Floyd, and she was duly discovered by Gilmour, becoming part of the male prog world. To her frequent mortification, Bush would see her record company, EMI, capitalize on her sexuality in various pin-up-style publicity shots. Paradoxically and otherwise, Kate Bush was one of the boys.

Although Bush would continue to use male session musicians throughout her career, the Fairlight meant she didn't always have to. Some were not happy about this. Thomson quotes *Never for Ever* keyboardist Max Middleton: "She had recorded this penny whistle which Paddy [Bush, Kate's brother] could play and then played it on the keyboard, and I thought it was a bit of a strange circle... Why not just play the pennywhistle?"[31] Guitarist Ian Bairnson was similarly disgruntled: "The technology was going quite wild at the time. I don't think she'd be upset if I said that at one point she was confused... There were four or five multi-track machines all loaded up and she had God knows how many tracks, she kept overdubbing things on it. It's that thing about having too much choice."[32]

If Bush had seen a room of her own in the Fairlight CMI during the recording of *Never for Ever*, she moved into that room for her next album, the ambitious 1982 digital-pop experiment *The Dreaming*. She had initially considered working with a few producers, including David Bowie collaborator Tony Visconti, but ended up producing the entire album herself. (Producer Hugh Padgham, whom Bush used on preliminary sessions for *The Dreaming*, departed after only three weeks.[33]) Bush hired session guitarists but used little of their work in the final product. Session musician Brian Bath speaks of *The Dreaming* as if it had erased him: "I just stepped aside in the end, I think I walked away... I felt a bit superfluous to what was going on. After five hours of playing the same bit you think, 'What do I do? Am I going anywhere, is anything happening?'"[34]

Something was definitely happening. The creative delving fostered by the Fairlight pushed daily recording sessions upwards of 20 hours during the late phases of *Never for Ever*,[35] but this was nothing compared to *The Dreaming*. Bush has described the period after *Never for Ever* as "a sort of terrible introverted depression."[36] Writing songs for *The Dreaming* brought her out of this depression, but a manic phase was to follow. As Bush moved into recording the album, she was loaned a Fairlight and then, near the end, purchased one for herself. Her relationship with the computer would not just aid but inform the album's concept and song structures. The computer was to become her, her art. When, seven years later,

Bush wrote "Deeper Understanding," a song about someone falling madly in love with their computer, she would speak from personal experience.

Initial tinkering with the Fairlight was akin to flirting. Bush's engineer on *The Dreaming*, Nick Launay, supported her as she developed a playful early process. "The fact that she was not quite in mastery of the technology was both thrilling and time consuming," writes Thomson, describing Bush and Launay "digging away" at *The Dreaming*'s songs, in the obsessive-compulsive, never-quite-done, limitless-archive-of-test-files way that digital technology abets. According to Thomson, the two often "[chased] their tails... ending up back where they started."[37]

Soon, Bush was neglecting her bodily needs. Although at the time she was known in the British media as a devoted vegetarian, active dancer, and sometime yogi, Bush was no health nut. She liked to chain-smoke while in the studio, for instance. "We were always sat in front of this desk, just me and her," remembers Launay of *The Dreaming*'s sessions. "And at the end of the desk there were two huge bars of Cadbury's milk chocolate and this huge bag of weed."[38] "Every night we ate take-away food," concurs Bush, "watched the evening news and returned to the dingy little treasure trove [i.e., the studio] to dig for jewels."[39]

By the time Bush got to the end of recording *The Dreaming*, she had hired engineer Paul Hardiman, who attests to the tight intertwining of Bush and the Fairlight. She was self-isolating, with the exception of her lover, the bassist and sound engineer Del Palmer. Thomson's version of the making of *The Dreaming* reads like a love triangle between Bush, Palmer, and the Fairlight, with, in the chain of erotic command, Bush reporting to the Fairlight, Palmer to Bush. "Del later talked about 'coming up' from the windowless basement studio as though they were on a submarine," writes Thomson.[40] Says

Hardiman: "Musicians were not around most of the time.... After their particular overdub was finished that was it until next time. The only constant was Del."[41]

In the durational final sessions for *The Dreaming*, "the fabric of reality started to warp and fray," according to Thomson.[42] Encouraged by the Fairlight's ability to mutate the recorded voice, Bush experimented with giving her singing a variety of tones straying from the willowy, girlish, "Wuthering Heights" soprano for which she had become known. Rerecording the master vocals in little sections that could then be digitally manipulated, Bush began screaming and grunting in the studio to give her voice texture, drinking milk and devouring chocolate bars to produce more mucous in her throat. The last two months of *The Dreaming*'s recording sessions coincided with the Falklands War. Bleak news reports came through TV screens on studio breaks, with Palmer worrying he would be conscripted.[43] By the end of the sessions, Hardiman claims Bush "was exhausted, and on nothing but a grape diet," working at least 15-hour days in the studio and then listening to rough takes afterwards and preparing for the next day's sessions, barely sleeping at all. "Even during meal breaks at the studio she would be tinkering with the Fairlight in the control room," writes Thomson. Bush: "When I come out of the studio, I feel like a Martian."[44]

Bush would speak of the recording of *The Dreaming* as "the hardest thing I've ever done... even harder than touring. It was worrying, very frightening."[45] The album itself is about worrying and frightening things. Its title track recounts colonial mining practices in Australia (where the Fairlight originates) that displaced Indigenous communities and ceremonies. Bush's self-isolation is the arguable motif of "All the Love," in which, inspired by a malfunctioning answering machine, she stitches together samples of the portion of messages in which her friends and family bid goodbye, as if she's not been heard from for days. Thomson suggests the lesson of *The Dreaming* can be found in a lyric from "Leave It Open," in which Bush growls through a processor, her voice sporadically played backwards as she becomes Faust and Mephistopheles at once: "Harm is in us."[46]

Bush took a six-month "rest cure" after making *The Dreaming*, by orders of her doctor father, who diagnosed her with stress and nervous fatigue. She had tried to go on vacation to Jamaica immediately after finishing the album, but it didn't work; it didn't switch anything off. "I went from this dingy little London studio with no windows to absolute paradise," Bush said. "I could barely stand it. Even the sound of the birds was deafening."[47]

The years following *The Dreaming* marked a now-celebrated period of self-determination for Bush. She would sing and write of attachment—love, lust, ambivalence, the pain of severance. A trilogy of albums, co-engineered by Palmer and recorded with him as the sole constant studio presence, loosely represents the phases of a long-term relationship: 1985's *Hounds of Love* (limerence, infatuation, loss of innocence), 1989's *The Sensual World* (co-dependence, finding and losing oneself in another, romantic failure), and 1993's *The Red Shoes* (saying goodbye). *The Sensual World*, about her disintegrating relationship with Palmer, was the last album on which Bush used the Fairlight. After *The Red Shoes*, at the point of the couple's break-up, Bush would not use the Fairlight again and not release another album for 12 years, although Palmer would return to assist on and co-engineer her comeback, *Aerial*. "I feel very relaxed with [Del]," Bush said to the press on *Aerial*'s release. "In some ways, in the nicest possible way, it's almost like he's not there."[48]

With his handsome, slender face and faded muttonchops, Palmer appears in the video for "Experiment IV" as one of the subjects of the musical technicians' search for a sound

Epilogue: Deeper Understanding

that "could kill someone from a distance."[49] We first see him in shadows, strapped to a chair and outfitted with wires. A little black box is placed on a plinth before him. The technicians retreat behind glass, playing sounds through the box to observe his reactions. A sound emerges from the box that soon materializes as what appears to be a sylph, played by Bush in a curly blonde wig. Bush-as-sylph blows Palmer a kiss, then pulls her face off to reveal a ghoulish skull and her true identity: a Banshee, the legendary female figure from Irish mythology who, like the Sirens, sings, or in this case shrieks, death. The video's POV shifts to this Banshee, and there is a fall-out in the secret bunker in which the experiment is being conducted, with most of the staff collapsing to the ground, dead or in shock, except one cloaked official who exits the bunker with the experiment's dossier. The last shot is of the official climbing into a van to make an escape. Their face is revealed: it's a winking Kate, putting a finger to her lips.

* * *

Only weeks after "Experiment IV" was released in 1986, the Irish actor Siobhan McKenna died. It was then, during the initial writing of *The Sensual World*, that Kate Bush likely first heard, or heard again, McKenna's recorded soliloquization of the character Molly Bloom's stream-of-consciousness monologue from the last chapter of the Irish author James Joyce's influential modernist novel *Ulysses*.[50]

Bush's encounter with McKenna's recording would form the basis of the song "The Sensual World," the initial version of which excerpted Molly's words verbatim. It would also form the basis of the album's centering of female experience. According to *The Sensual World*'s liner notes, Del Palmer programmed the album's percussion tracks on the Fairlight. As Bush worked through the album and, presumably, her break-up with Palmer, she would form a new relationship, a self-fashioned antidote, perhaps, to her encounter with the Fairlight during *The Dreaming*, when Palmer was her brother in arms.

The notoriously withholding Joyce estate would eventually forbid Bush from using Joyce's words directly in "The Sensual World."[51] So, Bush transposed the monologue in her lyrics, with a conceit about Molly "stepping out of the page" and "into the sensual world" seeming a response to the estate's censure—lines that would become the song's refrain and the album's name. In Joyce, Molly remembers her sexual encounters in a half-dream, fantasizing about what she might do apart from her husband Leopold (sucking pretty cocks that aren't his), mocking his sexual ineptitude while recalling their premarital bliss. "Yes" is the famous last word of *Ulysses*. It is Molly's word, Joyce's concept of the open feminine. In "The Sensual World," Bush adds an "oooo" before the yes—as if listening intently, in rapt dialogue.[52]

In October 1988, Bush met Trio Bulgarka for the first time, later noting the coincidence of the first letters of their first names spelling "YES"—Yanka Rupkina, Eva Georgieva, and Stoyanka Boneva.[53] Trio Bulgarka was not on the song "The Sensual World" but they, like Molly, represented an eminent encounter on the album. "I've never really worked with such hard-working professional people," Bush told BBC Radio One in 1989, "and I've never worked with women either, which I found fabulous. It was very exciting for me, working with women creatively."[54] If the Fairlight was Bush saying "yes" to independence, Trio Bulgarka was Bush saying "yes" to finally working with session musicians who were female.

Kate's world-music aficionado brother Paddy brought Trio Bulgarka to her attention in 1985.[55] Bush was over a year into recording *Hounds of Love*, on which her song "Jig of Life" featured a Bulgarian tapan drum. Bush wanted to collaborate but was shy to contact the Trio, who had contributed to the fetishized compilation album *Le Mystère des Voix Bulgares*, first released in 1975 and then rereleased in 1986 on the 4AD label, whose stable of bands such as the Cocteau Twins and Dead Can Dance seemed to have a numinous bond with ancient Balkan sounds. Bush did not want to fetishize further, did not want a collaboration to fail. After her resolve took over, she telephoned folk-music producer Joe Boyd, who had been working with Trio Bulgarka as part of the Bulgarian folk-music supergroup Balkana. Boyd and Bush made plans to meet Trio Bulgarka in Bulgaria's capital Sofia for the weekend.[56]

Although Trio Bulgarka appears elsewhere on *The Sensual World*, it is "Deeper Understanding" that is the probable reason why Bush, a nervous and infrequent traveller, made the pilgrimage to Sofia in the first place. As Bush told *Melody Maker* in 1989:

> When I was working on "Deeper Understanding," the idea was that the verses were the person and the choruses were the computer talking to the person. I wanted this sound that would almost be like the voice of angels: something very ethereal, something deeply religious, rather than a mechanical thing. And we went through so many different processes, trying vocoders, lots of ways of affecting the voice, and eventually it led to the Trio Bulgarka.[57]

A year earlier, in the *NME*, journalist Len Brown found Bush and Trio Bulgarka a week or so after the Sofia visit in a "broom cupboard" of a studio in Islington, London, aptly named Angel Recording Studios. The reclusive, private Bush was unprecedentedly letting the BBC film parts of the recording process for a TV program titled *Rhythms of the World*. Bush told Brown: "I wrote a track with a choir-synthesiser sound hoping that if we could get to work with them, they would take the weight of the song from the synthesisers." Later in the piece, Bush describes the "emotions" that are "translated" to a non-Bulgarian speaking listener as "very deep information."[58]

Bush's wish for the Trio to "take the weight of the song from the synthesizers" puts them in superficial counterpoint to the Fairlight. This is an untidy division. Bush would indeed see the Trio and the folk culture they represented as a useful tool, a new means by which to relate and create, to extend expression. She was not the only one.

Bulgarian singing has been understood by many non-Balkans through superlatives such as "emotional," "ethereal," "mystical," "haunting," "atmospheric." Many Western musicians have identified the music's effect as sublimely strong, an alien force, a salutary drug. Ex-Beatle George Harrison once gave Yanka Rupkina one of his records with an ardent, personalized dedication: "To one of the greatest singers on the planet."[59] On a 1980s radio show, Harrison said: "This is the kind of music that never reaches a lot of people because no one would ever play it but at the same time I think we'd be a much better world if everyone was forced to listen to it."[60]

It is distinctive of the Balkan region to sing in unusual (to Western ears) harmonic intervals, in the diaphonic style. One or more singers hold a single note, while the lead singer takes on a melody that frequently mixes dissonantly with the base note. As singers both amateur and professional know, holding a note powerfully, steadily, and in tune while another sings on top, dissonantly or not, takes both technical skill and strength of will. That Bulgarian singers tend to sing from an open, engaged throat rather than from the diaphragm, and that Bulgarian vocal songs, with breath control in mind, can stop abruptly and perfectly for a few seconds only to start again in booming pitch, make the music seem as bionic as it does "earthy."

Singing broke the ice on the Trio's first meeting with Bush and Boyd in Sofia, during which there were significant communication barriers apart from the spoken word. (A Western "yes" headshake means "no" in Bulgaria, and vice versa, cutely relevant in the context of "oooo yes.") Although the Trio brought Bush to tears as they sang, there was exacting work to be done, a kind of interfacing. Eva began by picking up the telephone to get her base note from the dial tone. Bush later told the BBC: "If you're in the same room as [the Trio] when they're singing, you can hear the air cracking... there's so much harmonic information in their voices."[61] Borimira Nedeva, a composer, musicologist, and translator who worked as a facilitator during *The Sensual World*'s Bulgarka sessions, felt "like a live electric wire, high-voltage currents running back and forth. I had to shoot words back and forth and see how they react and try to see what's good and try to promote it." Echoing comments made by male session musicians about Kate and the Fairlight, Nedeva confessed: "Sometimes Kate didn't know what she wanted."[62]

Unlike the Fairlight however, the Trio could not be stuck in a windowless studio to be tinkered with indefinitely. Bush had to work fast in Sofia on rudimentary arrangements and compositions, aided by Bulgarian arranger Dimitur Penev and state radio ethnologist Rumyana Tzintzarska, and then shortly afterwards in London, where long studio sessions were nonetheless markedly finite. Trio Bulgarka was accompanied to London by an "official translator," for instance, who was really there to ensure the women didn't defect from their communist home country.[63]

Bush would tell the *NME* of the "totally emotional" way she communicated with Trio Bulgarka. Like the mail-ordered program in "Deeper Understanding," the Trio offered something exceptionally, uniquely intimate. Said Bush to Brown:

> We can't talk intellectually. We can't talk about the state of Bulgaria or even what the shops are like in London. It's an incredible experience, the warmth they give you—you don't often get it from Westerners. Here it's very much a communication of "I have this, you don't have that" or "I don't have that and you do," whereas they want to know what kind of person you are. You can feel them probing your heart.[64]

In *Melody Maker*, Bush enthused that the Trio would "just come up and touch you and cuddle you, and you can go up and give them a big cuddle."[65] In a 1989 interview for WFNX radio in Boston, Bush again extols the cuddles, adding, "They're like my sisters now, I now have three sisters!"[66]

In her book *Performing Democracy*, Donna A. Buchanan, a specialist in music from Bulgaria, the Balkans, Russia, and the Caucasus, writes a chapter on the Bush–Bulgarka collaboration. Buchanan mentions in a footnote that she "was unable to locate the original arrangements from which the Trio sings excerpts" on any of the three songs on which they appear on *The Sensual World*.[67] "Just what the Trio was actually singing about was beside the point," Buchanan writes of "Deeper Understanding." "The texts were, in this piece, virtually undecipherable and the original sources unacknowledged."[68]

Irene Markoff, ethnomusicologist, instrumentalist, singer, and professor at Toronto's York University, tells me over email that she, likewise, could not discern any specific Bulgarian lines in "Deeper Understanding." "The lyrics in Bulgarian music are associated with the category/context of the songs," Markoff writes, identifying categories that loosely confirm Bush's attempt in "Deeper Understanding" to evoke something "primeval" (to use a qualified adjective of Buchanan's).[69] There are the rituals of the calendar, Christmas, Easter, and other pagan-inflected seasonal observances, work songs, and table songs (sung while drinking or eating); and there are the life-cycle rituals, from birth, to engagement and wedding, to death.

Weeks after *The Sensual World* was released, the Berlin Wall fell. The day after, long-time Bulgarian President Todor Zhivkov was deposed. According to Buchanan, selections from *The Sensual World* were aired on Radio Sofia and Bulgarian national TV on November 26, 1989, and March 3, 1990, respectively, the latter marking Liberation Day from Turkish rule, and in 1990 having, of course, double resonance.[70]

The notion that Bulgarian singing and folk culture in general represent resistance to oppression is not unusual in interpretations of the genre. Graeme Thomson quotes Nedeva as saying the Bulgarians under Ottoman rule "made nests of culture that couldn't be reached, and they preserved language, [identity], songs. It was absolutely isolated for 500 years, and these songs are sung in [that] old style."[71] In stressing Trio Bulgarka's angelic casting in "Deeper Understanding," Bush positioned Bulgarian music as a salve for trauma:

> And Bulgaria, the suffering that those people have gone through is tremendous... They were absolutely tortured, really, by the Turks. And I think the music reflects tremendous suffering. And comfort in music through suffering. Which I think is not unusual, that places in the world where people have a very, very hard time, normally the music is exquisite. Music is one of those few things that in very hard times people can hang on to. It can help people.[72]

Under Zhivkov, an insidious cultural campaign unfolded in Bulgaria, to which folk musicians like Trio Bulgarka were not entirely divorced. Turk, Roma, and Muslim names became "bulgarized" and by the mid-1980s, the Turkish and Romani languages were forbidden in public places, mosques were shut, and vocal opponents were sent to labour camps, with resettlement ongoing.⁷³ This state project, known by the Orwellian name *Vazroditelen protses* (alternately translated as "Revival Process," "Process of Rebirth," or "Regeneration Process") and defended as a response to centuries of Turkish rule, also involved the writing of new Bulgarian history books erasing Turkish presence, and an assembled team of academics whose own dubious experiment was to prove that Bulgarian Turks had always been Bulgarian, and had been forced to convert to Islam.⁷⁴ By 1989, Turkey had opened its borders expressly to Bulgarian Turks, effecting the forced emigration of hundreds of thousands Turks between May and August of that year. The government called it *Goliamata ekskurziia*, or the "Big Excursion"; others called it ethnic cleansing.⁷⁵

Meanwhile, so-called traditional music and dance had been deployed in Bulgaria to reinforce and proclaim the communist regime. Since the Ottoman Empire focused on colonizing towns and cities in Bulgaria, regional music represented by groups like Trio Bulgarka came, after liberation, to signify endurance of Bulgarian culture. In his book *Music in Bulgaria*, ethnomusicologist Timothy Rice notes that what had been "a communal and community activity" of dancing and singing in rural areas of Bulgaria became "a performing art with a sharp split between performers and audience," morphing into "a symbol of the Communist Party, the nation, and submission to Soviet domination in cultural, political, and economic matters."⁷⁶ Recording stars like Trio Bulgarka were part of this cultivation.

Under communism, Rice argues, Bulgarian folk music and dance were not just separated from the church and from their context in rural ritual but were also slicked up and recontextualized as the voice of the commoner, with generous state sponsorship (alongside science, literature, education). Bulgarian folk culture became an ironic means of touting something as new, future facing—if not invention, then re-invention.

As a technology of the state, Bulgarian music and dance were freighted with contradiction. At once, notes Rice, they were a way for rural workers who moved to cities during communism to maintain a connection with their homes. But they also bore traces of the kind of poverty and class exploitation the communist state desired to erase. Communism made folk music new by, Rice argues, arranging it in the Western-classical sense,

> adding chordal accompaniments and countermelodies to previously unaccompanied melodies; singing in choruses instead of solos or duets; playing in orchestras rather than solo or in small bands; dressing up in old-fashioned costumes for performances; and creating performance situations with a sharp split between the active performers and their passive audience.[77]

As Bush herself demonstrated with her Trio Bulgarka collaboration, business was booming in Bulgaria for a variety of innovative arrangers of folk culture.

The Bulgarian government invited Philip Koutev, a classical composer, to put together the State Ensemble of Folk Song and Dance, modeled after similar outfits in the Soviet Union.[78] Auditions were held for singers and dancers. What had been part of daily rural life became something like a reality-TV contest, in which the lucky, talented few would be "discovered" and perform for the state, nationally and internationally. (Travel abroad was rare during the communist era.) It was this Ensemble of Koutev's that appeared on a 1965 compilation album released by the US label Nonesuch that essentially introduced Bulgarian music to the West, to the likes of George Harrison, Paddy Bush and, ultimately, Kate Bush.

Trio Bulgarka contributed to the Bulgarian State Radio and Television Female Vocal Choir before collaborating with Bush. Their contemporary, Valya Balkanska, part of the Rodopa State Ensemble for Folk Songs and Dances, also left Bulgaria for professional purposes, but traveled even farther than they. In 1977, Balkanska's voice, singing a late 17th-century ode to a rebel leader, "Izlel je Delyo hajdutin" ("Delyo has become hajduk"), went into outer space on the Voyager Golden Record, two, 12-inch phonograph records made of gold-plated copper, carried on the probes Voyager 1 (currently the human-made object farthest from earth) and Voyager 2. Both records consisted of sounds from earth, and included Watlington's and Payne's whale songs—with all tracks selected by a committee chaired by author and cosmologist Carl Sagan. The records, on which Balkanska is one of the few female musicians, are intended to "communicate a story of our world to extraterrestrials,"[79] according to NASA. Former US president Jimmy Carter's dedication to the aliens: "This is a present from a small, distant world, a token of our sounds, our science, our images, our music, our thoughts and our feelings. We are attempting to survive our time so we may live into yours."[80]

* * *

During her 12-year hiatus between *The Red Shoes* and *Aerial*, Kate Bush appeared on the Prince song "My Computer." She sings back-up, but you wouldn't know it if not for the credits. Bush's voice, heavily processed, could be mistaken for a multi-tracked Prince, or a simulation. Bush had already collaborated with the US funk artist on "Why Should I Love You?" from *The Red Shoes*, which contains the lyrics, "The 'L' of the lips are open / To the 'O' of the host / The 'V' of the velvet / The 'E' of my eye."[81] If Bush had tried to posture as Prince through this velvet (oral sex?) reference, "My Computer" is Prince's effective update of "Deeper Understanding," its concept identical but newly situated in the late 1990s, when being social with one's PC was somewhat more banal.

Prince's song begins with an AOL sample ("you've got mail"). Like "Deeper Understanding," the song is written in the first person, yet Prince is clearly identified as its narrator. Prince presents a two-part case as to why, on a Sunday night, he has decided to "scan my computer looking 4 a site."[82] He's disappointed with the people in his life ("I can count my friends with a peace sign: 1, 2") and with the state of the world ("I have a child, I have a lot 2 explain"). Later in the song, Prince admits he's "got no mail" (presumably the occasion for the song, making its introduction an unsurprising corporate lie). The song ends, not with angels or birds, but with another AOL sample ("goodbye"). There is no transcendence.

In April 2011, Bush unveiled her own redux of "Deeper Understanding," the first and only single from *Director's Cut*, released a month later, which remixed and, in some cases, rerecorded songs or parts of songs from *The Sensual World* and *The Red Shoes*. ("Flower of the Mountain" allowed Bush to cast "The Sensual World" as it had been intended, its original lyrics finally endorsed by the Joyce estate, and so rerecorded, with Bush replacing her original "oooo yes" with the textually accurate if passionlessly pedantic "yes.") In an interview with *Pitchfork*'s Ryan Dombal promoting *Director's Cut*, Bush claimed to have "always been a big fan of analog."[83] The comment would be more shocking had Bush not released 2005's *Aerial*, which contained almost entirely organic sounds. In *Aerial*'s final song, the conceit of which feels like the end of an ecstatic acid trip in the British countryside, Bush, now a mother, positions herself as the eponymous contraption, "up on the roof,"[84] her body and mind the only technology she needs to tune into the sublime sounds of the universe she so blessedly inhabits.

When asked by Dombal about the initial reason for writing "Deeper Understanding," Bush says,

> I was working with the Fairlight, which was the first sampling machine and was actually quite the computer, though I tended to only use it on the surface. So I was around all this technology, and the song was about this contradiction of technology bringing a person more love and humanity than their own contact with actual people. Perhaps it's something that people can relate to more now because we all have computers in our own homes eating up our time.[85]

Pointing to mobile phones, Bush adds, "everyone is too busy, including me." Later she adds, "I love the sound of analog tape, but there's so many things you can do with [the music software] Pro Tools that would be incredibly difficult and very time-consuming with analog."[86] This, in response to Dombal's question about the computer's voice in the rerecorded "Deeper Understanding": instead of her own voice, Bush revisited the song using the autotuned voice of her 12-year-old son Bertie. "I could use a truly computerized voice that would stand alone," Bush says of the new "Deeper Understanding," only offering that she used Bertie instead because the computer is "meant to be a very kindly presence."[87]

In the Bush-directed video for the redone song, this is not exactly the case. The video itself represents the third version of "Deeper Understanding." For if the rerecorded version adds Bush's autotuned pre-teen son, tweaks lyrics subtly but significantly ("go execute" is gone), removes much of Trio Bulgarka and all of the final bird songs, and has an extended outro in which Bush scat-sings the original lyrics over a jamming harmonica while glitchy sounds interrupt as if the recording has digital indigestion, the video adds such a significant, confounding narrative to the original's lyrics that it becomes its own thing. The results are the revelation of an aesthetic malfunction.

The video stars actor Robbie Coltrane (aka *Harry Potter*'s Hagrid), who plays the protagonist coming home to his highrise apartment from work, his tie loosened, his shirt slightly rumpled. He sits in front of an iMac. He grabs a CD-ROM, the case of which has printed on it, in DS-Digital font, "VOICE CONSOLE: WHENEVER YOU NEED A FRIEND." There is a pair of smiling, red, lipsticked lips between title and subtitle. Coltrane puts the program in his iMac, and it starts: "Welcome to video console, the only one who really understands you."[88]

The red lips on the case begin to speak on his screen, reminiscent of the opening credits for *The Rocky Horror Picture Show*. Coltrane laughs (he is understood by the program) and also cries, put in a trance by this connection. His family barges in when Bush sings of his family intervening; they pull the plug on his computer. After they leave, Coltrane tries to fix the plug and it works: his beloved voice console is back, and she blows him a kiss, what looks like a red balloon full of water that meets his face, and pops.

Then the program crashes, and Coltrane can't get it to work again. Then, he is electrocuted through his efforts, passes out, and sees a white light. Then, he is on a Fellini-esque stage, holding a champagne glass and cheersing with friends and colleagues. Then, the stage turns into his apartment: everyone he's ever known is there. Then, his wife and children approach him and seem to want to offer love, but then, everyone points at him and laughs, including a clown. Then, after they turn their backs and walk away, he chokes and wakes up. Then, a coloured ball of light comes out of his mouth and begins to behave like a moth; it might contain a surveillance camera. Then, Coltrane tries to capture it but can't, and it soon flies out his window. Then, he follows it, wandering through the city streets. Then, he sees red cartoon sine waves coming out of an apartment window and follows them, after the ball of light emerges from his mouth again. Then, he breaks into the apartment and inside is a glam-rock programmer-cum-hacker, played by comedian Noel Fielding. This is the person behind the lips—or so it seems. Then, Coltrane kills Fielding by strangulation. Then, Coltrane approaches the computer with frenzied happiness, hoping to rekindle his relationship with the voice console.

There are a few ways this could end. The last shot of the "Deeper Understanding" video shows a screen with what appear to be Noel Fielding's eyes, peering over the program's smirking red lips—a "gotcha" reminiscent of the ending to the "Experiment IV" video. The lips must be Kate's.

Notes

Preface

1. Stuart Hall, "Gramsci and Us," in *The Hard Road to Renewal: Thatcherism and the Crisis of the Left* (London: Verso, 1988), 165.
2. Robert Wyatt, "The Age of Self," track 5 on *Old Rottenhat*, Rough Trade, 1985.
3. Hannah Arendt, *The Life of the Mind* (New York: Harcourt, 1978), 88.

Prologue: Some Radicals

1. Stan Douglas, "Introduction," in *Vancouver Anthology*, ed. Stan Douglas (Vancouver: Talon Books, 1991), 16.
2. Brian Pascus, "Activist Greta Thunberg Reaches New York after Sailing across the Atlantic," *CBS News*, August 28, 2019, https://tinyurl.com/3cdf6txa. NB. all websites were accessed September 2024.
3. News Staff, "Greta Thunberg Asks Media to focus on Other Young Climate Activists," *CityNews*, December 9, 2019, https://tinyurl.com/3bp6jyf9.
4. Stephanie Wood, "'Where Were You 10 Years Ago?' Musqueam Activist Asks Climate Strikers," *National Observer*, October 27, 2019, https://tinyurl.com/ye2a5556.
5. "Greta Thunberg Delivers Speech at Vancouver Climate Strike Rally," posted by CBC News, October 25, 2019, video, 4:14, https://tinyurl.com/y7scc9xe.
6. "Severn Cullis-Suzuki Speaking at Rio in 1992," posted by David Suzuki Foundation, June 12, 2012, video, 2:32, https://tinyurl.com/2ytareah.

7. "Can Young People Change the World?" December 20, 2019, in *The Real Story*, produced by BBC News World Service, podcast, 7:18, https://tinyurl.com/3ctbw8s7.
8. Ibid., 1:19.
9. Ibid., 11:15.
10. Judy Rumbold, "My Vile Bodies: Cindy Sherman Interview—Archive, 1991," *Guardian*, January 10, 1991, https://tinyurl.com/ymkbe369.
11. Ibid.
12. Ibid.
13. Ibid.
14. Hal Foster, "Obscene, Abject, Traumatic," *October* 78 (Autumn 1996): 118.
15. Valeriano Bozal, *Goya: Black Paintings* (Madrid: Fundación Amigos del Museo del Prado, 1999), 5, 6, and 55; see also Julia Blackburn, *Old Man Goya* (New York: Vintage, 2002), 40 [e-pub]; and Nigel Glendinning, "The Strange Translation of Goya's 'Black Paintings,'" *The Burlington Magazine* 117, no. 868 (July 1975): 465.
16. Glendinning, "The Strange Translation of Goya's 'Black Paintings,'" 466.
17. Ibid., 473.
18. Derek Allan, "The Death of Beauty: Goya's Etchings and *Black Paintings* through the Eyes of André Malraux," in *History of European Ideas* 42, no. 7 (2016): 4.
19. Ibid., 14–15.
20. See, for example, H.G. Wells, *The Conquest of Time & The Happy Turning: A Dream of Life* (Cornwall: House of Stratus, 2002), 7.
21. T.S. Eliot, *The Sacred Wood: Essays on Poetry and Criticism* (London: Methuen, 1976), 125.
22. David Graeber, "The Auto-Ethnography that Can Never Be and the Activist Ethnography that Might Be," davidgraeber.org, 2005, https://tinyurl.com/bdevew8j; and Edward Lucie-Smith, *The Decline and Fall of the Avant-Garde* (London: Cv Publications and Kindle Editions, 2013), 1.
23. See Lucie-Smith, *The Decline and Fall of the Avant-Garde*, 5.

24. Jed Rasula, "Make It New," *Modernism/Modernity* 17, no. 4 (2011): 718.
25. Rosalind Krauss, *The Originality of the Avant-Garde and Other Modernist Myths* (Cambridge, MA: MIT Press, 1986), 6.
26. Lawrence Rainey, "Introduction," in *Futurism: An Anthology*, eds. Lawrence Rainey, Christine Poggi, and Laura Wittman (New Haven, CT: Yale University Press, 2009), 7.
27. Krauss, *The Originality of the Avant-Garde and Other Modernist Myths*, 19.
28. Ibid., 17.
29. Judy K. Collischan Van Wagner, *Women Shaping Art: Profiles of Power* (New York: Praeger, 1984), 152.
30. Rachel Kushner, *The Flamethrowers: A Novel* (London: Random House, 2013), 119 [e-pub].
31. Jesse Barron, "Insurrection: An Interview with Rachel Kushner," *The Paris Review*, April 3, 2013, https://tinyurl.com/4k2xfkzy.
32. Rachel Kushner, *The Flamethrowers*, 91.
33. F.T. Marinetti, *The Founding and Manifesto of Futurism* (1909), in *Futurism: An Anthology*, eds. Lawrence Rainey, Christine Poggi, and Laura Wittman (New Haven, CT: Yale University Press, 2009), 53.
34. Antonio Sant'Elia, *Futurist Architecture* (1914) in *Futurism: An Anthology*, eds. Lawrence Rainey, Christine Poggi, and Laura Wittman (New Haven, CT: Yale University Press, 2009), 201.
35. Lawrence Rainey, "Introduction," 14.
36. Ibid., 29.
37. Ibid., 32.
38. John Ruskin, *Modern Painters by a Graduate of Oxford* (1843), vol. 1 (New York: John Wiley and Son, 1868), 90.
39. Rainey, "Introduction," 34.
40. Bonnie Marranca, "Ages of the Avant-Garde," *Performing Arts Journal* 16, no. 1 (January 1994): 9.
41. Richard Foreman, "Ages of the Avant-Garde," *Performing Arts Journal* 16, no. 1 (January 1994): 15–17.

42. Ibid.
43. The Rolling Stones, "As Tears Go By," track 9 on *December's Children (and Everybody's)*, Decca, 1965.
44. Marianne Faithfull with David Dalton, *Faithfull: An Autobiography* (New York: Cooper Square Press, 2000), 20.
45. Ibid., 21.
46. Sheila Weller, *Girls Like Us: Carole King, Joni Mitchell, Carly Simon—and the Journey of a Generation* (New York: Washington Square Press, 2008), 301.
47. Don Henley, "The End of the Innocence," track 1 on *The End of the Innocence*, A&M, 1989.
48. Billy Joel, "We Didn't Start the Fire," track 2 on *Storm Front*, Columbia, 1989.
49. Kevin EG Perry, "Grimes is Ready to Play the Villain," *Crack* online, April 29, 2019, https://tinyurl.com/37stsryx.
50. Ibid.

1. Culture Industry, Culture Wars

1. Edward Said, *Orientalism* (London: Penguin, 2003), 6.
2. Naomi Mezey, "Law as Culture," in *Cultural Analysis, Cultural Studies, and the Law: Moving Beyond Legal Realism*, eds. Austin D. Sarat and Jonathan Simon (Durham, NC: Duke University Press, 2003), 41.
3. Ibid., 42.
4. Max Horkheimer and Theodor W. Adorno, *Dialectic of Enlightenment: Philosophical Fragments*, ed. Gunzelin Schmid Noerr, tr. Edmund Jephcott (Stanford, CA: Stanford University Press, 2002), 18.
5. Ibid., 95–96.
6. Ibid., 98.
7. Ibid., 111.
8. Ibid., 104.
9. Ibid., 125.
10. Byung-Chul Han, *The Burnout Society*, tr. Erik Butler (Stanford, CA: Stanford University Press, 2015), 8.

11. Ibid., 2.
12. Mark Fisher, *Capitalist Realism: Is There No Alternative?* (Ropley, Hants: Zero Books, 2009), 3.
13. Han, *The Burnout Society*, 10.
14. Ibid., 13.
15. Ibid.
16. Max Horkheimer and Theodor W. Adorno, *Dialectic of Enlightenment*, 27.
17. Samantha Fox, "The Smiths: Panic (Rough Trade)," Review: Singles, *Smash Hits*, July 16–29, 1986, 61.
18. Hannah Arendt, introduction to Walter Benjamin, *Illuminations: Essays and Reflections*, ed. Hannah Arendt, tr. Harry Zohn (New York: Schocken Books, 2007), 11.
19. Walter Benjamin, "The Work of Art in the Age of Mechanical Reproduction," in *Illuminations: Essays and Reflections*, ed. Hannah Arendt, tr. Harry Zohn (New York: Schocken Books, 2007), 218.
20. Ibid., 221.
21. Ibid., 224.
22. Ibid., 236.
23. Ibid., 241.
24. Instrumental to this section is the overview of Hall's work in James Proctor, *Stuart Hall* (London: Routledge, 2004).
25. Stuart Hall and Paddy Whannel, *The Popular Arts* (Durham, NC: Duke University Press, 2018), 70.
26. Ibid., 197–198.
27. Stuart Hall, "Notes on Deconstructing 'The Popular,'" in *Cultural Resistance Reader*, ed. Stephen Duncombe (London: Verso, 2002), 186.
28. Ibid., 187.
29. Ibid., 188.
30. Ibid.
31. See Friedrich Nietzsche, *The Birth of Tragedy*, tr. Douglas Smith (Oxford: Oxford University Press, 2000).
32. Serge Gainsbourg, "Qui est 'in' qui est 'out,'" track 10 on *Initials B.B.*, Philips, 1968.

33. See Nancy Fraser, *The Old Is Dying and the New Cannot Be Born* (London: Verso, 2019), 12 [e-pub].
34. Ibid., 11.
35. See Tom Wolfe, *Radical Chic & Mau-Mauing the Flak Catchers* (New York: Picador, 1970).
36. Stuart Hall, "Encoding/Decoding," in *The Cultural Studies Reader*, 2nd ed., ed. Simon During (London: Routledge, 1999), 510.
37. Bob Marley and the Wailers, "War," track 9 on *Rastaman Vibration*, Island, 1976.
38. Stuart Hall, "Gramsci and Us," in *The Hard Road to Renewal: Thatcherism and the Crisis of the Left* (London: Verso, 1988), 167.
39. Margaret Thatcher, interview for *Woman's Own*, Thatcher Archive (THCR 5/2/262): COI transcript, Margaret Thatcher Foundation website, https://tinyurl.com/452fmpw6.
40. James Proctor, *Stuart Hall*, 58.
41. Stuart Hall, "Encoding/Decoding," in *The Cultural Studies Reader*, 2nd ed., ed. Simon During (London: Routledge, 1999), 508.
42. Ibid., 517.
43. Iryna Ja. Matsevich-Dukhan, "The 'Creative Turn' in European Social Theory," *Journal of the Belarusian State University. Sociology* 2 (2021), 47.

2. Natural Supernatural

1. Giacomo Leopardi, "Dialogo della moda e della morte" ("Dialogue between Fashion and Death"), in *Operette Morali: Essays and Dialogues*, tr. Giovanni Cecchetti (Berkeley, CA: University of California Press, 1982), 71.
2. Walter Benjamin, "Theses on the Philosophy of History," in *Illuminations: Essays and Reflections*, ed. Hannah Arendt, tr. Harry Zohn (New York: Schocken Books, 2007), 258.

3. Theodor W. Adorno, *Aesthetic Theory*, tr. Robert Hullot-Kentor (London: Continuum, 2002), 32.
4. Susan Bruce, "Introduction," in *Three Early Modern Utopias: Utopia, Atlantis, The Isle of Pines* (Oxford: Oxford University Press, 1999), xxi.
5. Michael North, *Novelty: A History of the New* (Chicago, IL: University of Chicago Press, 2013), 1.
6. Michael Schmidt, *The Novel: A Biography* (Cambridge, MA: Belknap Press, 2014), 11.
7. North, *Novelty*, 1.
8. Ibid., 2.
9. Eyal Weizman, "Walking through Walls: Soldiers as Architects in the Israeli–Palestinian Conflict," *Radical Philosophy* 136 (March/April 2006), 11 and 15.
10. Peter Bürger, *Theory of the Avant-Garde*, tr. Michael Shaw (Minneapolis, MN: University of Minnesota Press, 1984), 3.
11. Cathy Park Hong, "Delusions of Whiteness in the Avant-Garde," *Lana Turner: A Journal of Poetry and Opinion* 7 (November 2014), https://tinyurl.com/3pnhae52.
12. North, *Novelty*, 3.
13. Ibid., 7.
14. Ibid.
15. Terry Eagleton, *After Theory* (New York: Basic Books, 2003), 69.
16. Ibid., 72.
17. North, *Novelty*, 18.
18. Ibid., 19.
19. Ibid.
20. Pliny the Elder, from *The Elder Pliny's Chapters on the History of Art*, tr. Katherine Jex-Blake, in *Art and Its Histories: A Reader*, ed. Steve Edwards (New Haven, CT: Yale University Press, 1999), 100.
21. Benvenuto Cellini, from *The Autobiography of Benvenuto Cellini*, tr. George Bull, in *Art and Its Histories: A Reader*, ed. Steve Edwards (New Haven, CT: Yale University Press, 1999), 109.

22. E.H. Gombrich, from "Norm and Form: The Stylistic Categories of Art History and their Origins in Renaissance Ideals," in *Art and Its Histories: A Reader*, ed. Steve Edwards (New Haven, CT: Yale University Press, 1999), 73.
23. Ibid.
24. Ibid.
25. Ibid., 74.
26. Ibid., 75.
27. Ibid., 74.
28. Ecclesiastes 1:9–10 (AV).
29. North, *Novelty*, 20.
30. Matthew 9:15–16 (AV).
31. II Corinthians 5:17 (AV).
32. Colossians 3:9–11 (AV).
33. North, *Novelty*, 45.
34. Hannah Arendt, *On Revolution* (London: Penguin, 1990), 45.
35. North, *Novelty*, 36.
36. Ibid.
37. William Shakespeare, *The Tragedy of King Lear*, in *The Riverside Shakespeare* (Boston, MA: Houghton Mifflin, 1974), 1.i.90.
38. Tom Wolfe, *The Painted Word* (New York: Bantam, 1976), 60.
39. Malcolm Gladwell, *Blink: The Power of Thinking Without Thinking* (London: Penguin, 2005), 296 [e-pub].
40. Ibid., 297.
41. David W. Galenson, *Old Masters and Young Geniuses: The Two Life Cycles of Artistic Creativity* (Princeton, NJ: Princeton University Press, 2006), 4.
42. Brainpickings.org is no longer online. Popova's mission statement remains widely quoted however, for example, Robert Rodriguez Jr., "Five Things I'm Enjoying Right Now," *Robert Rodriguez Jr.: Inspiring the Creative Spirit* (blog), August 21, 2015, https://tinyurl.com/4x3prbh5.
43. See, for example, "Creativity is a Renewable Resource," *Art Center of the Bluegrass* (blog), June 22, 2021, https://tinyurl.

com/2k9567wp (accessed September 2024); and Harish, "Timeless Creative Inspiration: 13 Ways to Jump Start Your Creativity," *Launch Your Genius* (blog), April 12, 2013, https://tinyurl.com/4w7svzj2.
44. Naomi Klein, *This Changes Everything: Capitalism vs. the Climate* (London: Penguin Random House, 2014), 250 [e-pub].
45. North, *Novelty*, 51.
46. Christopher Hitchens, *God Is Not Great* (New York: Hachette Book Group, 2007), 255 [e-pub].
47. Charles Darwin, *On the Origin of Species by Means of Natural Selection, or the Preservation of Favored Races in the Struggle for Life* (New York: D. Appleton and Co., 1861), n.p.
48. Ian Hacking, "Introductory Essay," in Thomas S. Kuhn, *The Structure of Scientific Revolutions*, 4th ed. (Chicago, IL: University of Chicago Press, 2012), 27 [e-pub].
49. Arthur Danto, "The Artworld," *The Journal of Philosophy* 61, no. 19, American Philosophical Association Eastern Division Sixty-First Meeting (October 15, 1964), 582.
50. George Dickie, "What is Art? An Institutional Analysis," in *Aesthetics: A Comprehensive Anthology*, ed. Steven M. Cahn, Stephanie Ross, and Sandra L. Shapshay, 2nd ed. (Hoboken, NJ: John Wiley and Sons, 2020), 430.
51. Mark Holsworth, "Danto's Art World (not an institution)," *Black Mark: Melbourne Art & Culture Critic* (blog), March 25, 2020, https://tinyurl.com/3hvkx6nj.
52. Thomas S. Kuhn, *The Structure of Scientific Revolutions*, 4th ed. (Chicago, IL: University of Chicago Press, 2012), 61 [e-pub].
53. Thomas S. Kuhn, "Postscript," in *The Structure of Scientific Revolutions*, 4th ed. (Chicago, IL: University of Chicago Press, 2012), 310 [e-pub].
54. Kuhn, *The Structure of Scientific Revolutions*, 72.
55. North, *Novelty*, 119.
56. Ibid., 120.
57. Dickie, "What Is Art?" 431.

58. Kuhn, *The Structure of Scientific Revolutions*, 91.
59. Ibid., 95.
60. Ibid., 266.
61. North, *Novelty*, 121.
62. Kuhn, *The Structure of Scientific Revolutions*, 246.
63. Ibid., 181.
64. Ibid., 266.
65. Said, *Orientalism*, 116.
66. Ibid.
67. Andrew Sullivan, "Is There Still Room for Debate?" *New York* magazine *Intelligencer*, June 12, 2020, https://tinyurl.com/2fskhxp4.
68. North, *Novelty*, 124.
69. Ibid.
70. Kuhn, *The Structure of Scientific Revolutions*, 265.
71. Ibid., 266.
72. Boris Groys, *On the New*, tr. G.M. Goshgarian (London: Verso, 2014), 130 [e-pub].
73. Hannah Gadsby, *Nanette*, directed by Madeleine Parry and John Olb (2018; Los Gatos, California: Netflix), 34:21.
74. Georg Wilhelm Friedrich Hegel, *Introductory Lectures on Aesthetics* (London: Penguin, 1993), 61.
75. Ibid., 13.
76. Groys, *On the New*, 3.
77. Ibid., 10.
78. Ibid.
79. Ibid., 43.
80. Ibid., 47.
81. Ibid., 52.
82. Ibid., 84.
83. Ibid., 107.
84. Ibid., 119.
85. Ibid., 120.
86. Ibid., 128.
87. Ibid., 158.

3. The Whole Earth

1. Tina Brown, *The Vanity Fair Diaries: 1983–1992* (New York: Henry Holt and Co., 2017), 76.
2. Andreas Reckwitz, *The Invention of Creativity*, tr. Steven Black (Cambridge: Polity Press, 2017), 15 [e-pub]. See also Richard Florida, *The Rise of the Creative Class: And How It's Transforming Work, Leisure, Community and Everyday Life* (New York: Basic Books, 2002).
3. Reckwitz, *The Invention of Creativity*, 8.
4. Ibid., 32.
5. Serge Guilbaut, *How New York Stole the Idea of Modern Art: Abstract Expressionism, Freedom, and the Cold War* (Chicago, IL: University of Chicago Press, 1983), 6.
6. "Federal Art Project of Works Progress Admin," *The Art Story*, https://tinyurl.com/yckhh9z.
7. Guilbaut, *How New York Stole the Idea of Modern Art*, 17–18.
8. Ibid., 21.
9. Ibid., 29.
10. Ibid., 31.
11. Ibid., 32.
12. Ibid., 36.
13. Clement Greenberg, "Avant-Garde and Kitsch," in *Art and Culture: Critical Essays* (Boston, MA: Beacon Press, 1989), 4.
14. Ibid., 8.
15. Ibid., 11.
16. Ibid.
17. Ibid., 7 and 19.
18. Ibid., 12.
19. Guilbaut, *How New York Stole the Idea of Modern Art*, 36.
20. Ibid., 38.
21. Clement Greenberg, "The Late Thirties in New York," in *Art and Culture: Critical Essays* (Boston, MA: Beacon Press, 1989), 230.
22. Guilbaut, *How New York Stole the Idea of Modern Art*, 42.

23. Mary Anne Staniszewski, *The Power of Display: A History of Exhibition Installations at the Museum of Modern Art* (Cambridge, MA: MIT Press, 1998), 159; see also Marcel Duchamp, "The Richard Mutt Case," *The Blind Man* 2 (May 1917), 5.
24. Staniszewski, *The Power of Display*, 78.
25. Guilbaut, *How New York Stole the Idea of Modern Art*, 45.
26. Staniszewski, *The Power of Display*, xxii.
27. Guilbaut, *How New York Stole the Idea of Modern Art*, 67.
28. Ibid., 55.
29. Staniszewski, *The Power of Display*, 4.
30. Ibid., 3.
31. Ibid., 14.
32. Ibid., 16 and 23.
33. See Mark Twain, *The Innocents Abroad* (London: Penguin, 2002).
34. Staniszewski, *The Power of Display*, 25.
35. Ibid., xxviii.
36. Ibid., 70.
37. Guilbaut, *How New York Stole the Idea of Modern Art*, 67.
38. Ibid., 68.
39. Ibid., 76.
40. Ibid., 62.
41. Ibid., 138.
42. Ibid., 136.
43. Ibid., 151.
44. Ibid., 86.
45. Ibid., 118.
46. Ibid.
47. Danto, "The Artworld," 580.
48. Guilbaut, *How New York Stole the Idea of Modern Art*, 185.
49. Ibid., 186.
50. "Interviews with Lee Krasner," in *Jackson Pollock: Interviews, Articles, and Reviews*, ed. Pepe Karmel (New York: Museum of Modern Art, 1999), 28.
51. Guilbaut, *How New York Stole the Idea of Modern Art*, Fig. 14.

52. W. Jackson Rushing, *Native American Art and the New York Avant-Garde: A History of Cultural Primitivism* (Austin, TX: University of Texas Press, 1995), xi.
53. Ibid., 6.
54. Ibid., 14.
55. Ibid., 23.
56. Ibid., 21.
57. Ibid., 26.
58. Ibid., 28.
59. Ibid., 30.
60. Ibid., 34.
61. Ibid., 36.
62. Ibid., 37.
63. Tina Loo, "Dan Cranmer's Potlatch: Law as Coercion, Symbol, and Rhetoric in British Columbia, 1884–1951," *Canadian Historical Review* 73, no. 2 (1992): 128.
64. Rushing, *Native American Art and the New York Avant-Garde*, 98.
65. Ibid., 99.
66. Ibid., 100.
67. Ibid., 103.
68. Ibid.
69. Ibid., 109.
70. Ibid., 108.
71. Ibid., 114.
72. Ibid., 115.
73. Ibid., 118.
74. Ibid., 121.
75. John D. Graham, *System and Dialectics of Art* (New York: Delphic Studios, 1937), quoted in Rushing, *Native American Art and the New York Avant-Garde*, 123.
76. Rushing, *Native American Art and the New York Avant-Garde*, 126.
77. Ibid., 161.
78. Ibid., 170.
79. Calvin Tomkins, *Duchamp: A Biography* (London: Chatto & Windus, 1997), 116.

80. Ibid., 143.
81. Ibid., 329.
82. Ibid., 344.
83. Calvin Tomkins, *The Bride and the Bachelors: Five Masters of the Avant-Garde* (New York: Gagosian, 2013), 67 [e-pub].
84. Ibid., 246.
85. Ibid., 247.
86. Ibid.
87. Elsa Schiaparelli, interview in *Harper's Bazaar*, May 1935, in *Schiaparelli & Prada: Impossible Conversations*, eds. Andrew Bolton and Harold Koda (New York: Metropolitan Museum of Art, 2012), 84.
88. Ibid.
89. *Sex and the City*, season 3, episode 17, "What Goes Around Comes Around," directed by Allen Coulter, written by Darren Star and Candace Bushnell, featuring Sarah Jessica Parker, Kim Cattrall, Kristin Davis, aired October 8, 2000, streaming on Crave, Canada, 4:18.
90. Ibid., 4:43.
91. Ibid., 9:36.
92. Hanisha Besant, "The Journey of Brainstorming," *Journal of Transformative Innovation* 2, issue 1 (2016): https://tinyurl.com/yexwfu3p.
93. Alex F. Osborn, *Applied Imagination: Principles and Procedures of Creative Problem-Solving*, 3rd ed. (New York: Charles Scribner's Sons, 1963), 15.
94. Ibid., 11.
95. Ibid., 12.
96. Reckwitz, *The Invention of Creativity*, 51.
97. Ibid.
98. Ibid., 52.
99. Ibid.
100. Ibid.
101. Pamela M. Lee, *Think Tank Aesthetics: Midcentury Modernism, the Cold War, and the Neoliberal Present* (Cambridge, MA: MIT Press, 2020), 13.
102. Ibid.

103. See, for example, Larissa MacFarquhar, "What Money Can Buy," *New Yorker*, December 27, 2015, https://tinyurl.com/yu3perrw.
104. Vannevar Bush, "As We May Think," *The Atlantic*, July 1945, https://tinyurl.com/5n7n5csm.
105. Lee, *Think Tank Aesthetics*, 13.
106. Ibid., 7. See also Sharon Ghamari-Tabrizi, *The Worlds of Herman Kahn: The Intuitive Science of Thermonuclear War* (Cambridge, MA: Harvard University Press, 2005), 46 and 61.
107. Lee, *Think Tank Aesthetics*, 15.
108. Ibid.
109. Ibid., 16.
110. Esther Dyson, George Gilder, George Keyworth, and Alvin Toffler, "Cyberspace and the American Dream: A Magna Carta for the Knowledge Age" *Future Insight*, Release 1.2 (August 1994), https://tinyurl.com/mr3rt39a.
111. Norbert Wiener, *Cybernetics: Or Control and Communication in the Animal and the Machine* (Cambridge, MA: MIT Press, 2019).
112. Jack Burnham, "Systems Esthetics," *Artforum* 7, no. 1 (September 1968): https://tinyurl.com/7am5n8wv.
113. Ibid.
114. Ibid.
115. Ibid.
116. Mary Anne Staniszewski, *The Power of Display*, 278.
117. Ibid., 269.
118. Ibid., 276.
119. Ibid., 270.
120. Kynaston McShine, "Essay," *Information* (New York: Museum of Modern Art, 1970), 139.
121. Tomkins, *The Bride and the Bachelors*, 104.
122. Ibid., 147–148.
123. Ibid., 175.
124. Ibid., 188.
125. Ibid., 190.
126. Burnham, "Systems Esthetics."

127. For McLuhan on tribalism, see, for example, *Understanding Media* (Berkeley, CA: Gingko Press, 2013), 40 [e-pub]; see also, Marshall McLuhan and Quentin Fiore, *War and Peace in the Global Village* (New York: Bantam, 1968).
128. McLuhan and Fiore, *War and Peace in the Global Village*, 11.
129. Philip Marchand, *Marshall McLuhan: The Medium and the Messenger* (Cambridge, MA: MIT Press, 1998), 237–239.
130. Margaret O'Mara, *The Code: Silicon Valley and the Remaking of America* (New York: Penguin, 2019), 129 [e-pub].
131. Jenny Andersson, *The Future of the World: Futurology, Futurists, and the Struggle for the Post-Cold War Imagination* (Oxford: Oxford University Press, 2018), 4.
132. Yuval Noah Harari, *Homo Deus: A Brief History of Tomorrow* (New York: Penguin Random House, 2015), 325.
133. O'Mara, *The Code*, 192.
134. Alvin Toffler, *Future Shock* (New York: Bantam, 1970), 111 [e-pub].
135. Ibid., 113.
136. Esther Dyson, *A Design for Living in the Digital Age* (New York: Broadway Books, 1997), 3.
137. Naomi Klein, *The Shock Doctrine: The Rise of Disaster Capitalism* (New York: Henry Holt & Co., 2007), 6.
138. Robert Hughes, *The Shock of the New* (New York: Alfred A. Knopf, 1980), 190.
139. Jodi Dean, *Blog Theory* (Cambridge: Polity Press, 2010), 15 [e-pub].
140. Ibid., 24.
141. Ibid.
142. Ibid., 37.
143. Ibid., 38.
144. Turner, *From Counter Culture to Cyber Culture*, 56.
145. Ibid., 57.
146. Ibid., 58.
147. Ibid., 61.
148. Ibid., 69.

149. Quoted in Katherine Fulton, "How Steward Brand Learns," *Los Angeles Times*, October 30, 1994, https://tinyurl.com/5374wjxh.
150. Turner, *From Counter Culture to Cyber Culture*, 81.
151. Mark Anthony Wilson and Bernard R. Maybeck, *Architect of Elegance* (Layton, UT: Gibbs Smith, 2011), 166; and "History," *Exploratorium* (online), https://tinyurl.com/4mf569nm.
152. "Aspects of Demise: The Whole Earth Demise Party," *Media Burn: Independent Video Archive*, https://tinyurl.com/3s29ryhd.
153. Turner, *From Counter Culture to Cyber Culture*, 101.
154. "Aspects of Demise: The Whole Earth Demise Party," 6:20.
155. Ibid., 2:38.
156. Turner, *From Counter Culture to Cyber Culture*, 102.
157. O'Mara, *The Code*, 97.
158. Ibid., 43.
159. Ibid., 180.
160. Ridley Scott, "1984 Apple's Macintosh Commercial (HD)," posted by Mac History (YouTube), February 1, 2012, video, 0:54, https://tinyurl.com/r7sskcmd.
161. Turner, *From Counter Culture to Cyber Culture*, 141.
162. Ellen Ullman, *Close to the Machine: Technophilia and Its Discontents* (San Francisco, CA: City Lights Books, 1997), n.p.
163. Ibid., 1.
164. Ibid., 110.
165. Ibid., 84.
166. Ibid., 40.
167. Ibid., 47.
168. Ibid., 45.
169. Ibid., 47.
170. Ibid., 49.
171. Ibid., 50.
172. Ibid., 136.
173. Ibid., 105.
174. O'Mara, *The Code*, 197.

175. Tsunami, "Kidding on the Square," track 20 on *World Tour & Other Destinations*, Simple Machines, 1995.
176. Ibid.

Epilogue: Deeper Understanding

1. Kate Bush, "Moving," track 1 on *The Kick Inside*, EMI, 1978.
2. D. Graham Burnett, *The Sounding of the Whale: Science and Cetaceans in the Twentieth Century* (Chicago, IL: University of Chicago Press, 2012), 635.
3. "Slowed-Down Solo Whale," produced by Roger Payne, recording by Frank Watlington, track 2 on *Songs of the Humpback Whale*, CRM Records, 1970.
4. Kate Bush, "Deeper Understanding," track 6 on *The Sensual World*, EMI, 1989.
5. Bush, "Deeper Understanding."
6. Katie Rife, "Kate Bush Invents the Internet with 'Deeper Understanding,'" *AV Club*, April 17, 2015, https://tinyurl.com/3pyhe729.
7. Wikipedia, "Internet Addiction Disorder," last modified September 16, 2024, https://tinyurl.com/5bmuf94v.
8. Steve Sutherland, "The Language of Love," *Melody Maker*, October 21, 1989, hosted by *Gaffaweb*, https://tinyurl.com/jek5bmtn.
9. See, for example, Bruce McDonald, WFNX Boston, "Interview with Kate Bush," Fall 1989, hosted by *Gaffaweb*, https://tinyurl.com/4kf6r9dh.
10. See, for example, James Essinger, *Jacquard's Web: How a Hand-Loom Led to the Birth of the Information Age* (Oxford: Oxford University Press, 2004).
11. See, for example, Ken Stieglitz, *The Discrete Charm of the Machine: Why the World Became Digital* (Princeton, NJ: Princeton University Press, 2019), 138.
12. See, for example, Andrew Holt, *Religion and World Civilizations: How Faith Shaped Societies from Antiquity to the Present* (London: Bloomsbury, 2023), 184 and 264.

13. Katy Waldman, "Reading Ovid in the Age of #MeToo," *New Yorker*, February 12, 2018, https://tinyurl.com/yjakccdn.
14. Claire L. Evans, *Broad Band: The Untold Story of the Women Who Made the Internet* (New York: Penguin, 2018), 15 [e-pub].
15. Ibid., 56.
16. Ibid., 57.
17. Ibid., 55.
18. Kate Bush, "Experiment IV," track 10 on *The Whole Story*, EMI, 1986.
19. See Paul Harkins, "Introduction" and Part I, *Digital Sampling: The Design and Use of Music Technologies* (London: Routledge, 2019).
20. Robert Fink, "ORCH5, or the Classical Ghost in the Hip-Hop Machine," in *Listen Again: A Momentary History of Pop Music*, ed. Eric Weisbard (Durham, NC: Duke University Press, 2007), 234.
21. "Herbie Hancock – Fairlight CMI – Rockit," posted by Ari Sawyer-Brooks (YouTube), March 30, 2011, video, 7:39, https://tinyurl.com/r7sskcmd.
22. "Kate Bush—Experiment IV—Wogan," posted by sunsetz777 (YouTube), January 7, 2012, video, 0:46, https://tinyurl.com/2xdr3thh.
23. Estelle Caswell, "The Sound that Connects Stravinsky to Bruno Mars," *Vox*, May 17, 2018, https://tinyurl.com/5n2dzxt3.
24. Graeme Thomson, *Under the Ivy: The Life and Music of Kate Bush* (London: Omnibus, 2017), 186 [e-pub].
25. Ibid.
26. Ibid., 187.
27. Ibid., 188.
28. Ibid.
29. Ibid.
30. Ibid.
31. Ibid.
32. Ibid., 189.
33. Ibid., 204.

34. Ibid., 206.
35. Ibid., 189.
36. Ibid., 198.
37. Ibid., 207.
38. Ibid.
39. Ibid., 211.
40. Ibid.
41. Ibid.
42. Ibid.
43. Ibid.
44. Ibid.
45. Ibid., 212.
46. Ibid.; and Kate Bush, "Leave It Open," track 5 on *The Dreaming*, EMI, 1982.
47. Thomson, *Under the Ivy*, 236.
48. Ibid., 365.
49. "Kate Bush—Experiment IV—Official Music Video," posted by KateBushMusic (YouTube), January 3, 2011, video, https://tinyurl.com/5ykf3dmf.
50. Siobhan McKenna, "Soliloquy of Molly Bloom," side 1 on *James Joyce, Ulysses: Soliloquies of Molly and Leopold Bloom read by Siobhan McKenna and E.G. Marshall*, Caedmon Records, 1960.
51. Thomson, *Under the Ivy*, 277.
52. Kate Bush, "The Sensual World," track 1 on *The Sensual World*, EMI, 1989.
53. Thomson, *Under the Ivy*, 300n.
54. Roger Scott, interview with Kate Bush, BBC Radio One, October 14, 1989, hosted by *Gaffaweb*, https://tinyurl.com/2s3rny78.
55. Thomson, *Under the Ivy*, 272.
56. Ibid., 274.
57. Sutherland, "The Language of Love."
58. Len Brown, "Down at the Old Bul' and Bush," *New Musical Express*, November 12, 1988, hosted by *Gaffaweb*, https://tinyurl.com/56by5veu.

59. Ilka Dimitrova, "Yanka Rupkina: Strandja Songs are my Life, Salvation, the Symbol of Bulgaria," *Radio Bulgaria*, October 9, 2016, https://tinyurl.com/n7jcw35t.
60. "Rockline w/ Bob Coburn—2/10/88 George Harrison Interview—Part 2 of 2," posted by Rich Marino (YouTube), December 18, 2016, video, https://tinyurl.com/5h5jmvjw.
61. Scott, interview with Kate Bush, BBC Radio One.
62. Thomson, *Under the Ivy*, 282.
63. Ibid.
64. Brown, "Down at the old Bul' and Bush."
65. Sutherland, "The Language of Love."
66. McDonald, "Interview with Kate Bush."
67. Donna A. Buchanan, *Performing Democracy: Bulgarian Music and Musicians in Transition* (Chicago, IL: University of Chicago Press, 2005), 382n.
68. Ibid., 381–382.
69. Irene Markoff, email interview with the author, August 21, 2019.
70. Buchanan, *Performing Democracy*, 383.
71. Thomson, *Under the Ivy*, 273.
72. Interview with Kate Bush, source unknown, in Seán Twomey, "Kate Bush Fan Podcast Episode 31—The Trio Bulgarka and Kate," *Kate Bush Fan Podcast*, July 5, 1990, MP3 audio, 17:05.
73. Tomasz Kamusella, *Ethnic Cleansing During the Cold War: The Forgotten 1989 Expulsion of Turks from Communist Bulgaria* (New York: Routledge, 2019), 41 and 102.
74. Ibid., 24.
75. Ibid., 8nn.
76. Timothy Rice, *Music in Bulgaria: Experiencing Music, Expressing Culture* (Oxford: Oxford University Press, 2003), 60.
77. Ibid., 62.
78. Ibid., 63.
79. "The Golden Record," *NASA* (online), https://tinyurl.com/47ypz72b.

80. Jimmy Carter, "Voyager Spacecraft Statement by the President, July 29, 1977," *The American Presidency Project* (online), https://tinyurl.com/3dxzedfn.
81. Kate Bush, "Why Should I Love You?" track 11 on *The Red Shoes*, EMI, 1993.
82. Prince, "My Computer," track 9 on disc 3 of *Emancipation*, NPG/EMI, 1996.
83. Ryan Dombal, "Kate Bush: The Elusive Art-Rock Originator on her Time-Traveling New LP, *Director's Cut*," *Pitchfork* (online), May 15, 2011, https://tinyurl.com/27xdhpe2.
84. Kate Bush, "Aerial," track 16 on disc 2 of *Aerial*, EMI, 2005.
85. Dombal, "Kate Bush."
86. Ibid.
87. Ibid.
88. "Kate Bush—Deeper Understanding—Official Video," posted by KateBushMusic (YouTube), April 25, 2011, video, https://tinyurl.com/4z2b8ywc.

The Pluto Press Newsletter

Hello friend of Pluto!

Want to stay on top of the best radical books we publish?

Then sign up to be the first to hear about our new books, as well as special events, podcasts and videos.

You'll also get 50% off your first order with us when you sign up.

Come and join us!

Go to bit.ly/PlutoNewsletter